Straight
From The
Heart

Straight From The Heart

True Stories of Remarkable Encounters With Once-In-A-Lifetime Horses

Compiled by the editors of EQUUS magazine
Foreword by Ami Shinitzky

Illustrations by Pamela Wildermuth

FLEET STREET PUBLISHING

Fleet Street Publishing
656 Quince Orchard Road, Suite 600
Gaithersburg, MD 20878

———————————————

Library of Congress Catalog Card Number: 97-76777
ISBN: 0-9611314-4-6 (PB)
0-9611314-5-4 (PC)

Acknowledgments

This anthology contains the works of 29 natural storytellers, many of whom could not have imagined how deeply their tales would touch our hearts. It also reflects our recognition, after 10 years of publishing the True Tales column, that these stories deserve a more lasting monument than a fleeting appearance in a monthly magazine.

The difficult challenge of selecting these stories from the many that have appeared in EQUUS was ably met by Julie Beaulieu, Teddi Lawrence, Laurie Prinz and Mary Kay Kinnish. Mary Kay also served as the capable chief editor for the entire project. The design of the book is the work of EQUUS' talented art director, Celia Strain.

Many thanks also go to the following people for their tireless efforts in taking this project from planning stages to finished product: Valerie Donohue, Carolyn Sutterfield, Jack Moore, Karen Du Teil, Sandy Oliynyk, Allison Rogers, Beth Wenger, Midge Johnson, Anup Samanta, Mark Haller, Bobby Byram and, last but not least, Sue Laden.

Table Of Contents

CHAPTER 3

Forever Transformed

CHAPTER 4

Chance Encounters

Foreword

Straight from the heart, and no less than pure magic. If ever the statement that life is more amazing than fiction is true, the tales that follow will absolutely convince you of it. And if you are a horse lover to boot, then as you marvel, laugh and cry reading these remarkable accounts, you'll repeatedly be reminded why you cannot imagine life without horses.

The place of horses in all human endeavors is accepted without much thought. For millennia, they have been an engine of agriculture, a weapon of war, a conveyer of people and a partner in competition. They have taken us to the ends of the earth and on parade down the street. They have been the subject of legends, of poetry and of art. They have delighted the hearts of children and been the source of immeasurable pride of staid men. They have been plain, noble and even with wings and a horn. They are woven into our lives no less than the sun and the moon and the seasons of the year.

But why have they become such a part of us? There are other beasts of burden, other of God's creatures who could serve man's needs, yet none other could ever take the horse's place. None other could capture and fill our hearts as horses have. None other has that nearly mystical quality that resonates so profoundly with so many of us. None other has...well, yes, embraced us as we have embraced the horse.

No matter the nature of our involvement with horses, they enrich our lives and are the source of fond memories and countless stories. From the joyous first gallop to the night-long vigil spent with a colicking horse. From the rogue who only love could tame to the incredible, breathtaking sight of the birth of a foal. Although no man or woman who has come in contact with a horse is ever at a loss for words when recalling an equine moment, many have been moved to weave some darn good tales. And that, some 10 years ago, gave me an idea.

The mission of EQUUS magazine is to speak about and for the horse—a focus that naturally has attracted readers who have a particularly strong bond to horses. Let's invite them, I reasoned, to send us unique episodes from their equestrian lives which the magazine would publish under the banner "True Tales." So we put the call out. Simple enough and more wonderful than I ever imagined. We received more than good tales; month after month readers created inspired prose that didn't fail to evoke in us a stir of emotions and grateful appreciation. I never could have guessed that ordinary folk, not professional writers, could produce such powerful work. Thank their horses, they would probably say.

This volume is dedicated to the many readers who have found the muse within them, put pen to paper and shared their personal moments with the EQUUS editors. They, in turn, selected one each month for publication in what has become one of the most popular features in the magazine. It was not an easy task to choose from nearly 100 published True Tales the remarkable 29 that follow. Some great ones, alas, have been left out.

As we hurl forward into the silicon age, where language is reduced to 0s and 1s and where emotions are merely something that clutters equations, let these tales remind you of a threatened and precious dimension of life. Ponder the mystery of the human-equine bond, and may you find sanity and respite within it.

Ami Shinitzky
EQUUS Founding Editor
Gaithersburg, Maryland
September 1997

CHAPTER 1

Unexpected Rewards

The Beauty Of An Ugly Horse

What Seabiscuit lacked in looks,
she more than made up for in natural ability and
willingness to please.

C.A. COLEMAN

She was by far the ugliest horse I had ever seen, and the first comment I directed toward her was "get rid of that one. Now."

We had just purchased our dream guest ranch in Idaho, although back then the place consisted of only an abandoned jumble of broken-down fencing, half-collapsed storage sheds, strewn garbage, rusty, obsolete machinery and six of the sorriest-looking animals on earth. The former owner, not eager to pour any more money into upkeep, had left the property in the middle of winter. The horses had been fending for themselves, and it was now up to us to get everything into shape for the approaching guest season.

The two Belgian geldings, whom we later used to pull wagons carrying visitors, had fared the best because their stature allowed them to reach high into trees, stripping bark and dead leaves. Two little black mules had survived by digging under the snow. A long-legged bay mare, immediately named Killer for her furious manner toward the others, was very much on the skinny side but survived to become my English riding horse. Regardless of our move into the middle of nowhere, I was determined to keep that pleasure in my life.

Then there was Seabiscuit.

Her real name was Rosie, but by the time someone who was familiar with her bothered to tell us, she'd been called Seabiscuit for so long that we never bothered to switch. One of our crew, who grew fond of her that first summer, had given her the name. I sarcastically called her Fleabag, regardless of his protests that she was a darn good horse.

I hadn't gotten over the annoyance of having her around, for right from the start, my wise husband, Tony, had insisted we keep her because, quite simply, we needed her. "Besides," he'd protested, "there isn't a thing wrong with her. She's sound. Dudes can handle her. Who cares if she isn't so pretty?"

"Not pretty" was an understatement in my book. That horse was a disgrace to the equine race. I had grown up on a dainty, beautifully colored Appaloosa-Thoroughbred, a show animal who placed in halter classes each time she entered the ring. People used to stop me as they saw her, exclaiming over her Arab-type head, arched neck and silver-gray hide, and with those memories and standards vivid in my mind I simply could not accept any ugly horses in our string—which grew to number 26 over the years, Seabiscuit included.

What was it that I disliked about her? To begin with, she had a horrible head, roman-nosed and parrot-mouthed, with eyes that protruded slightly from their sockets. A crooked white blaze, starting over her left eye and ending over her right nostril, gave her a lopsided air—I was constantly tempted to get some paint and a brush and fill out the mark so that it looked more even.

She had a ewe neck, high withers and a backbone that looked like it could rake you through the saddle leather. She was cow-hocked in the hind legs, slightly pigeon-toed in the front and had a chest space so small that it seemed out of place on an adult animal. I avoided her religiously, riding every other horse and mule available instead. It seemed to me that for a person to look good when riding, the animal had to be halfway decent, too.

Then one day I had to ride old Fleabag. We had spotted some renegade cattle in our meadow, and I was in need of the first herder I could get my hands on. I jumped on and soon discovered she had a mouth like a brick wall. Once she got wound up with the shouting, rein slapping and mad galloping required in such circumstances, I found it nearly impossible to stop her from running with me into Montana. Afterward, the difficulties with her only made me mock her more.

The following summer, after a year of the good feed, regular dewormings and groomings shared by all our stock, Seabiscuit shed out from a dull brown to a deep red, complete with a gloss that arena competitors would have sold themselves for, and her mane and tail became thick and wavy. Running with the herd, she looked and acted like a graceful yearling (we'd figured her to be around 20), and her muscle tone improved to the point where even I had to admit, reluctantly, that she had nice hindquarters. She went back into active duty that season, hauling kids, parents and our crew over mountain paths, across cold, rushing streams and over fallen logs. Tie her up for hours when the lake trout were biting hard, and she wouldn't move beyond shifting her weight as she dozed. Offer her a carrot or apple, which people often did after reaching into the depths of their lunch bags, and she would accept it thoughtfully and with dignity, never coming close to a finger. Everyone loved and raved about her—several in particular even talked about taking her home with them.

"Seabiscuit?" I'd say. "Are you kidding?"

Then came the day when my own chosen mount broke loose from his tie during the night, leaving me with seven hours of rugged trail to cover, on foot, before getting home. With a low stockpile of supplies remaining after our week's worth of camping, Tony was able to switch both panniers and riding-pack saddles around to come up with a substitute. As I was rolling up the last foot of my bedroll, he came up to me leading the ugly mare. She was wearing my saddle and bridle, and I could only stare at him, open-mouthed.

"I can't ride that!" I was finally able to protest, under my breath so that the guests wouldn't hear. "I can't be seen on that horse!" In response I got Seabiscuit's lead rope. "You have no choice," he answered softly. "She's all that's available right now."

I hadn't quite settled on her back before I heard a camera click: One of the guests had happily taken my picture. "I see you're riding your favorite animal!" he teased, having heard me making fun of her earlier on the trip. "How's she feel?" "Awful!" I called back, just as gleefully, although grumbling to myself. And Seabiscuit lowered her head and fell into line with all the others.

That ride through the awesome Idaho wilderness, first along the mighty Salmon River, then up a lengthy series of switchbacks to the mountain "breaks," then gradually down the other side to our ranch, with elk and deer bounding out of our way and the sun gradually burning off the morning chill, was the most humbling experience of my lifelong horse career, something that taught me more than any riding lesson, book, fellow horseman or personal experience ever had and, I believe, ever will. It amazed me, impressed me and, much later, when we were all safely back in the corral with supper smells floating across the yard, caused me to sincerely apologize to an animal I'd both misunderstood and grossly misrepresented.

Seabiscuit was wonderful!

She was a smooth, steady mount, slowing down around tight turns and taking tiny, precise steps on steep ascents. She did not bite at the horse in front of her, nor kick at the one in back. She watched the trail calmly, yet alertly, not even reaching for a clump of grass unless we had stopped for the necessary rest periods. Never had I felt so safe and well cared for—Seabiscuit needed neither guiding nor correcting, because she was so sure of her own natural abilities. To this day, that memory both thrills and hurts me. I had been so prejudiced by her appearance, I hadn't given her the chance to show me her real worth.

For four months, I sought out Seabiscuit whenever I needed a horse I could count on. She was one of the few who would leave the herd behind and, all alone, carry her rider without balking, looking back, whinnying or trying to turn around. Once, after a severe thunderstorm, she and I discovered a huge tree down across a flat section of the wagon path. Rather than return home that moment for a chain saw to cut it up, we decided to get a running start and jump it. I expected some awkwardness, but my mount cleared the obstacle easily, with so much grace and perfection that for hours afterward I blissfully daydreamed about turning her into a professional. Of course, when stroked and praised, she looked back with a sort of mild surprise that rebuked me slightly for ever doubting her at all.

I tried all sorts of bits to stop her occasional head tossing, but it took a teeth-floating session for us to discover the real basis of her discomfort. "Look at this," Tony said, as he reached for her tongue, and when I stepped up for a closer look, I was sickened.

Her tongue was twisted and mangled and much too short for her mouth, looking as though it had nearly been severed at one time and, left without medical care, had healed incorrectly. Tony released her tongue, and Seabiscuit gratefully took a step back, not comfortable with having it handled. Looking from Tony, who was shaking his head, to the mare, I wondered how on earth this had happened and who was responsible. My heart ached. Afterward, I switched to a mechanical hackamore, and she liked it much better.

Tony and I went on a long vacation that winter, driving back to

Ohio to visit with his parents, then taking a trip to Alabama to sightsee with mine. All told, we were away from home just over a month, but as we'd hired what we'd thought were competent, knowledgeable caretakers, we had no fears or doubts. None at all.

Much later, from a concerned neighbor who had been called to the ranch right after the accident happened, we learned that one of the employees had decided to go riding to alleviate boredom, even though this had been forbidden in our absence. She had urged Seabiscuit into a canter in a section of meadow that was riddled with ground-squirrel holes (for years we had kept up a steady but losing battle against the rodents). Seabiscuit had fallen, and her rider had tumbled off.

When we first arrived home, we found the mare holed up in the yard, dirty, forlorn and limping so badly from a sore left hind leg that she could barely make it in and out of the barn. "She fell going to the creek for water with the others," the young wife had hastened to explain at the time. "Oh, poor thing! Chip and I were barely able to get her back in here!" Indeed, the mare was in great pain, although her dark eyes were quiet when we looked her over. Nothing was broken, nothing was swollen and there was nothing wedged in her hoof wall. What especially puzzled us was how she'd fallen in the first place when we'd never even known her to stumble.

We checked the path to the creek for ice, and found it so well-traveled that any patch that might have made it slick had already been broken into pieces by the 25 sets of hooves going back and forth daily. We walked the snow-covered trails made by the horses, finding nothing hidden that could have caught her off guard. We questioned the caretakers over and over, still unsuspicious, even when they announced they had another job waiting and had to leave. And we called our veterinarian, a three-hour drive away, to see if we could make an appointment.

After listening to our description of her condition, he told us that Seabiscuit most likely had either a sprain or a spavin. He advised waiting to see if she improved. "If she doesn't," he suggested, "you could turn her into a broodmare."

Suddenly, the idea of having a foal out of Seabiscuit seemed like the perfect idea, one we should have thought of long ago. In May we took her to a gorgeous Quarter Horse stallion, leaving her for two cycles. It was a gamble, we felt, but knowing healthy, well-cared-for mares could safely carry and deliver into their late 20s, we felt we had to try.

All summer long, we watched her like hawks. Again she grew glossy. She continued to run with the herd, although sideways, her bad leg held out. She grew fat, then fatter, and with joy we told each other that even in her advanced age, Seabiscuit would not let us down. "Come on, Seabiscuit," I often whispered when I saw her. "Let us keep you. Please let us keep you."

The former owner of the ranch turned up again at this point. He had some more horses he wanted to sell. One of them, he said, was Seabiscuit's last colt. We eagerly asked him how old the youngster was. "About five," was his answer, "I think."

We bought Clyde, a small-boned bay with no white, about a week later. He didn't look much like his mother—in fact, he was actually handsome and well put together. I was disappointed: The only resemblance was the black mane and tail. "Her next foal will be more like her," we hoped aloud.

The next foal never came. We waited until November to haul Seabiscuit out for a pregnancy test, wanting the baby to have as much growth advantage as possible. Our veterinarian is good, but we didn't want him to palpate too soon and, by some long shot, misdiagnose. As it stood, he felt around inside our mare for five, long, agonizing minutes before he slowly removed his gloved hand. "She's open" was all it took to bring tears to my eyes.

He had already looked at her still-bad leg, announcing that surgery was our only route. It would be expensive, he warned, and she still wouldn't be good as a trail horse. Considering her age, it seemed too much for her to have to go through. Tony and I stood looking at each other as he spoke. Rosie, alias Seabiscuit, and lately called Babe with a great deal of affection, was never to be useful again.

Now Tony and I were faced with the single most horrible decision we'd had to face in our married lives. Would we be able to feed a nonworking animal that winter and into the future, when our budget was so strict that our already-stored hay and grain were practically worth their weight in gold? Could we justify keeping an expensive pet who would always need painkillers, hot pads and other special care? Worse, could Seabiscuit withstand another harsh winter, even in a stall in the barn, in mountains where temperatures often hit 30 below and snow fell for weeks at a time? Finally, was it fair to the rest of our horses to cut back on their time with us—moments when we brushed them, cleaned their hooves, checked them for cuts and bruises and in general just hugged and talked to them?

The veterinarian read our thoughts and, with the professional detachment that such people develop over time, suggested having her put down. "She's had a long life and a happy one with you folks," he said, softening at our stricken faces. "It would be a lot kinder than letting her suffer every day for the remainder of her time." I looked at Seabiscuit, who was starting to doze off, and past images of her flashed through my heart. The tears were now falling in earnest, and I didn't bother to wipe them away.

I don't think it's necessary to tell the end of Seabiscuit's story, for anyone who has ever loved and respected a horse and had to say good-bye knows how the memories linger, sometimes unbearably. At the time she left us, I did love and respect that patient, big-hearted, surefooted and beautiful animal, while simultaneously feeling the guilt that comes with having once rejected a being on the basis of appearance alone.

Six months ago, at a sale, Tony bought a pinto mare with a "white" eye and huge, paddle-like hooves. He liked her sturdy look, he said, and the way she moved in the arena. I said she looked eerie with that funny eye, but I test-rode her anyway. You know, she's a real gem. When I watch her playing with the others in the meadow during their days off, I am glad Tony brought her home. Of course, she reminds me of Seabiscuit—the most beautiful ugly horse I'll ever have the pleasure to know.

A Horse For All Seasons

*How a klutzy Quarter Horse named Jake
taught a lesson to last a lifetime.*

SHELBY WEEKS

Certainly every horse owner has a favorite story that demonstrates how his horse taught him an unforgettable lesson. For me, the horse was Jake, a klutzy, red-dun Quarter Horse who happened into my life by coincidence and taught me the value of looking through the exterior of a being to see the essence of beauty within.

Jake's beginnings were pretty humble. He was born in a back-yard to a Quarter Horse mare who had met briefly with a locally well-known stallion. From the start, Jake seemed to be one of those horses who would never grow into his bones. He was terribly accident-prone. Before he was six weeks old, he was badly cut by barbed wire. The episode left him with a fist-sized hole in his neck that never quite filled in, although the hair grew back. Jake left his first owner with a veterinary bill that wasn't quite covered by the price paid for him by a neighbor's teenage daughter.

Polly was hopeful that her new acquisition would eventually do well as a Western pleasure horse. She spent a lot of time over the next two years teaching the gelding the basics of halter showing and Western riding. She also spent a good bit of money having the veterinarian stitch him up again and again. Soon after Polly bought Jake, a herdmate kicked a hole in his side. The spot remained for some time and never completely returned to normal. With that, plus the chunk missing in his neck, Jake was starting to look dented. At two, he nearly gutted himself on a wooden fence post. That episode left him with a 38-inch scar that stretched from the barrel across his hip to his dock. After that, the veterinarian suggested that Jake be kept in a box stall.

For a few months, solitary confinement worked well. By the time Jake celebrated his third birthday, he had reached his full height of 16.2 hands. Although that was tall for a Western pleasure horse, he managed to win some halter classes at the local horse shows. Then one night while he was alone in his stall, Jake inexplicably broke his face. The left side was pushed inward and the sinus and eye socket were damaged. The eye, miraculously, was fine. But even after the veterinarian spent hours putting the broken bones back in place, the left side of Jake's face looked very different from the right side.

When that injury finally healed, Polly decided to sell Jake. She had no reason to hope that the accident-prone horse would ever become less of a financial drain, and she was already certain that he would never be the slick pleasure horse she wanted, considering all of his scars and dents.

Polly tried to sell the gelding in the usual ways: by word of mouth and through advertisements in the newspaper and notices at the local tack shop. The few lookers who came out left almost as soon as Jake stuck his head out of the stall. At last, with the board due, the veterinary bill overdue and no offers, Polly sent Jake to the local horse auction. There, he was sold for 56 cents a pound to an agent for a Canadian slaughterhouse.

Right about the same time as Jake was being prepared for his long journey to Canada, his veterinarian happened to mention the unfortunate loss of his best equine patient to Lt. Col. F.W. Townsley (U.S. Army-retired), who, for the first time in his 65 years, found himself without a horse. For some reason, he was intrigued by the story of the horse with the broken face, so he called a horse trader he'd done a lot of business with and asked him to find Jake for him. Fourteen telephone calls later, that man managed to find where the gelding was being kept. With a borrowed trailer, Lt. Col. Townsley drove three hours to the holding area. He made a deal with the agent, and Jake was his. The gelding had missed boarding the truck to Canada by less than an hour.

Lt. Col. Townsley, or Sam, as I have the privilege of calling him, had earned his first horse, Queenie, when he was five years old by washing dishes for a year on his family's Massachusetts farm. During World War II, Sam served with Gen. George S. Patton in Europe. In Austria, he was field captain of the USA Forces Jumping Team. He won the International Jumping Trophy in 1958 at Innsbruck, Austria. When he was transferred to Japan, Lt. Col. Townsley became a lifetime member of the Palace Riding Club and a member of the Imperial Jumping Team of Tokyo. Once back in the United States, he participated in the Three-Day Wofford Cup in Colorado Springs, and at Fort Leavenworth he became joint master of the Fort Leavenworth Hunt and president of its board of governors.

After he retired from the military in 1962, Sam Townsley joined the faculty of Culver Military Academy in Culver, Indiana. As a senior instructor and head of the horsemanship department, he was responsible for buying and selling horses to maintain a riding herd of 100 black horses and 38 polo ponies. Fourteen years later, he retired once again, and Jake was the horse he chose to keep him company.

In all of Sam's years with horses, one aspect had been delightfully absent from his experience with them. Not since before he had joined the military had he ever had to care for his own horse. He was accustomed to allowing others to do the mundane chores and present his groomed mount, outfitted with a clean saddle and bridle, whenever he wanted to ride. Try as he might, Sam wasn't sure he would ever be able to totally care for Jake, so he inquired about bringing his new horse to my farm. I agreed to board Jake in exchange for riding lessons.

Soon I was washing two years' worth of mildew fungus from the finest saddles and bridles I had ever seen. Some of the equipment had been given to Sam as awards; some he'd bought in Europe; all of it was first-rate.

Every day Sam came to work with Jake. He spent much of the first week fitting different bridles on the gelding, trying different cavessons and bits. He tried two different saddles with three different pads and four different girths before he settled on a satisfactory combination. He kept up a quiet conversation with me and the horse, explaining the theory of each thing he was doing as he worked around him. About the fourth day, he longed Jake and pronounced him ready to ride. Sam still had riding privileges at Culver Military Academy, so we hauled Jake there.

In the great riding hall, longer and wider than a football field, the autumn sun filtered through the tall, narrow windows. There Sam began to retrain Jake while I watched. They began by walking in slow perfect circles that used exactly half of the arena. Then they reversed and walked in slow perfect circles using the other half of the hall. Along the walls, where the wainscot sloped inward to prevent any stirrup from marring the hall's interior, were letters that designated quadrants. At times, I suspected that Jake had learned to read them.

As Sam and the gelding worked, my lessons began, too. First, Sam explained the five rein effects and how each was used. He cited authors of old cavalry manuals and the published works of his teachers, as well as his own theories of riding. As the weeks passed, the walked circles gave way to trotted figure eights and eventually became cantered figure eights with graceful flying lead changes. The riding lasted about two hours. For 15 minutes Sam warmed up with circles at a walk. For an hour he practiced the invisible, inaudible aids he used to move Jake smoothly from one gait to the next. And for 15 minutes, he asked Jake to try something new—a shoulder-in or countercanter or a turn on the forehand or the hindquarter. When the gelding performed the new maneuver, Sam stopped the lesson and cooled Jake off with 15 or 20 minutes of walking in circles.

In the beginning, as I watched them work together, I saw what I thought was a great waste. The superb riding master with his elegant equipment and so many years of knowledge was frittering away his time and mine on a beaten-up nag. After a few months, however, I realized that Jake was being transformed. The droopy-headed Western pleasure horse with the shuffling gaits was gone. In his place was a light-footed, arched-necked, wonderfully responsive horse who, at times, appeared to dance to music that only he and his rider could hear. With no perceivable cues, the gelding trotted in place, flashed an extended trot or trotted diagonally. The same was true at a canter.

For the hour that they worked hard, the only sounds were Sam's soft words of encouragement to Jake and the rhythmic beat of Jake's hooves. The solitary man on the solitary horse weaved magically through imaginary mazes in the silent hall. And Jake was beautiful. From the tip of his flaring nostrils to the arch of his waving tail, every muscle seemed to strain to respond to the motionless man astride him. The scarred body and the misshapen head were hidden by the perfect harmony between horse and rider.

In January, Sam pronounced Jake ready to jump and asked if I would be the gelding's rider. Years ago, Sam's knee had been broken in a fall from a hunter and the old injury was aggravated by jumping. Jake and I learned to jump together since my previous experience was limited to cow-hopping an Arabian over a hay bale. The first time Jake saw cavalletti, he dropped his nose and picked his way over them like a true trail pony. But once he got the idea that he was supposed to go over and through a jump, nothing was too high or too wide.

Culver Military Academy had an unlimited supply of standards and bars, faux-brick blocks, rustic elements, cavalletti and coops available for the indoor arena. Outside were oxers and sheep pens, ditches, banks, drops and water spreads. That winter Jake and I jumped them all. Some days he jumped spreads and some days in-and-outs. On others, he worked on height or perhaps took a full course of various jumps. But Jake jumped only three days a week. The other three he worked with Sam on the flat. Sundays, we all rested.

In the spring, Sam and I showed Jake in jumping classes, where appearances didn't count, and he won many times. I showed him in adult classes, and one of Sam's former students flew from Boston to show Jake in junior division. That summer, Sam turned down three offers for Jake—one of which was five times his purchase price. In the fall Jake foxhunted, and in the winter he refined his jumping skills. The second spring, he again had a successful show season. By outward appearances, Jake looked to be a fine jumper, a dependable hunter and a consistent winner in English pleasure classes, even if he was a bit scarred.

Yet the gelding's finest moment was not in the show ring nor on the hunt field. From somewhere deep inside, a genetic memory of some long-dead Quarter Horse ancestor stirred within him. In the presence of only a handful of witnesses, Jake did something he'd never been trained to do.

One July evening, Sam stopped by with Sweeney, a South

African who had attended the academy. He was a small man dressed in shirt, tie and a leather hat with a zebra-tail hatband that ended in a long black tassel.

As conversations do, this one wandered until I mentioned The Cow. Living in my back 80 was a Hereford who had gone wild. Turned out as a calf with 50 other cows three years ago, she refused to be caught when the others were brought in in the fall. Recently she had calved, and now the joke around the neighborhood was that in a few years I would own an entire herd of feral bovines. Sweeney asked why I didn't rope The Cow and her calf. I explained that while roping was quite common in the West, I knew of no one in the state of Indiana who could rope a cow from horseback. Sweeney pushed his hat back and said that he could do it if he had a horse. Sam offered Jake.

A call to the neighbors located a Western saddle, and from his luggage Sweeney pulled a zebra-hide bag and produced a rope. Then the quiet South African took off his tie, rolled up his shirt sleeves and tucked his trouser legs into his boots. He drew on well-worn gloves and stepped outside to shake out his loop.

I put Jake in his usual egg-butt snaffle, but instead of his usual saddle pad, I folded an old bedspread under the neighbor's stock saddle. If Jake sensed something different, he didn't show it. I handed the gelding's reins to Sweeney. He patted the horse and then checked every point of the rigging with great care. He adjusted the stirrups and mounted in one quick motion. I opened the gates to all of the connecting fields, and Sweeney cantered away, standing in the stirrups, looking for The Cow.

The two had no sooner disappeared over a rise, when they thundered back. Frantically dodging and twisting in front of them was The Cow's tiny, white-faced calf. Low on Jake's neck, Sweeney leaned forward, swinging a loop. The gelding was hardly recognizable as the refined jumper I knew. His reins hung free on the saddle horn, his big, ugly head was only inches from the ground, and he dodged and twisted seconds before the calf, effectively driving it through the gate into the pasture in front of the house where we all stood. Directly in front of us, Sweeney threw a small, tight loop and wrapped the free end of the rope around the saddle horn. The calf hit the end of the rope. Jake stopped. As the calf tried to scramble to his feet, Sweeney was off Jake, working down the rope. But the gelding, with no training at all, backed steadily, keeping the rope taut. Only when Sweeney had tied the calf's feet with a short strap he had carried in his teeth did Jake take three steps toward him and free the rope.

Then they went after The Cow.

It took three hours.

The Cow was a fierce, clever, determined beast. She had watched Sweeney catch her calf and all of us load him into a truck. Then she took off for the woods. Sweeney and Jake tried to drive her into the open so Sweeney could rope her. She was big, but very fast. Yet slowly, losing two feet for every three they gained, Sweeney and Jake worked The Cow toward the front of the house, where we waited. With one smooth throw, Sweeney settled the rope around The Cow's neck. Jake dug in and nearly sat down to offset the bone-jarring jerk as the 800-pound cow hit the end of the rope. Sweeney was almost thrown from the saddle when The Cow flipped into the air and crashed to her side. She lunged to her feet, desperately circling Jake. No matter what direction she went, Jake kept the rope taut and faced her. Sweeney sat with his arms folded on his chest, letting the big horse show his stuff.

Eventually, with help from the spectators who had gathered, The Cow and calf were safely sent to my neighbor's farm. Sweeney packed up and hurried to catch a plane to South Africa. And Jake went back to the showring and the hunt field.

After another year, I moved away and Jake's daily care fell to a new rider named Marilyn Coby. She refined her jumping skills with Sam and Jake, and frequently used the gelding to demonstrate jumping techniques to the Marshall County 4-Hers who attended clinics put on by Sam and Jake. Then Sam was in the hospital for a while, and the gelding was put out to pasture although he was only eight. A couple of years passed. Sam called me in June and said he'd been out to see Jake. It looked to him as though the horse was lonesome. Sam asked me to keep Jake until he was up to riding him again, and I agreed. Last weekend, my daughter showed Jake. If she felt embarrassed by his bizarre appearance, she never showed it.

They brought home five blues.

This Girl's Life

*The adventures of a budding equestrian
as seen through the eyes of her mother.*

VIRGINIA TENER BOFMAN

"All she needs is some kind of a Western hat and maybe a kerchief around her neck. She'll sit up on my horse, and we'll lead her around the arena," said my husband, Ralph, enthusiastically describing his plan for our daughter's equestrian debut. "It's called the Tom Thumb class for tots her age."

He volunteered to outfit Tina, who was then just about three years old. They returned with a straw Western hat, all right, but instead of a kerchief, they had gone in for the whole ensemble: a bright Western shirt, whipcord Western pants and tiny Western boots. The bill was $40. Not much now, but in 1952, it seemed like a fortune! I was furious. Of course, Tina looked just darling perched on that big palomino, and she loved it. She waved, she smiled, she won. And that simple little horse show is what complicated my life for years.

We lived in Sacramento, California, near the Land Park pony rides. Guess who was their best customer? We knew the location of every merry-go-round for miles, we could shop only at markets that had coin-operated mechanical horse rides, and every drive down a country road meant pointing out horses. Tina had stuffed horses, horse figurines, horse pictures. Her world was hemmed in by horses, I thought. But Ralph assured me that there was no need to worry; Tina would grow out of it. Gradually, I would hear him using the name of a horse in vain: "You do this, and I'll buy you a horse." "If you're not a good girl, I won't buy you a horse." We talked, mostly I talked, but nothing changed.

Almost five years slid by. We moved from Sacramento to the Rock House, the roadhouse from Hell, 21 miles east of Oroville on the Feather River Canyon Highway. There Ralph would surely make his fortune: It had everything—bar, restaurant, motel, service station and boardinghouse. Oroville Dam construction was just starting, and workers filled the canyons. "What a great place to keep a horse," Ralph said, and from then on, I lost all arguments. However, the horse never materialized. All Tina ever heard was more promises.

Then the totally unexpected happened: Ralph had a fatal car accident. Tina, not yet nine, and I were left alone in the Rock House. She loved her daddy, and in a desperate effort to cheer her up and keep her occupied while I ran the business, I succumbed and bought her a horse.

Would that I could back up and live this little portion of my life over again. Once Smokey entered our lives, things were never the same. She was a 15-year-old bay mare about 14 hands tall, and I think I paid $150 for her. Smokey had a sweet disposition and lots of patience. Nobody ever taught Tina to ride; she just knew how. From the first time she sat in that old McClellan saddle, rider and horse took to each other immediately. They were like one.

The men living at the boardinghouse and in a nearby trailer park watched all this develop. Where to keep Smokey? Not to worry. The men got together and, using the trees for fence posts, had a corral ready in no time, followed by a lean-to shelter and a feed bin. What would we feed her? I never lacked for advice: "If that were my plug, I'd turn her out in that little meadow and let her eat all the green grass." "No matter what you do, don't let her eat all that green grass, she'll get colic." And on it went. Once a big truck loaded with alfalfa lost its brakes on the hill near our place. You guessed it. Over it went, and everyone in the county was down there carrying off hay. All the tunnel stiffs and customers jumped into their pickups and brought back enough feed for months. (I want you to know that this was in 1957, before the law about recovering salvage from wrecks went into effect.)

We occasionally had other memorable little episodes. Like the day when, at high noon with the restaurant full of people, the phone rang: "Missus, your horse is down on the highway, and some car is going to run into her." The phone call at 1 a.m.: "Your mare is up here wandering around in the trailer park." Off I'd go, leaving a bar full of people and stumbling up the hill in the dark to catch that damn horse. One busy afternoon: "Missus, your little girl is chasing my cattle and running off all their weight. I'm going to shoot that blankety-blank horse if you don't come and stop her."

Then my mother came to visit: This was a big mistake. Judging from her moaning that she never expected to see her daughter "in a place like this" and fretting about her darling grandchild "running wild on a horse," Mother didn't have a very good time. Neither did I. I had just dressed Tina (under protest) in a pretty, new princess-style dress of pink polished cotton. She had pink bows in her ponytail and lace on her pink socks. I wanted her grandmother to see what a perfect little lady she was, but where was she? We went outside to look around, and here came Tina, bareback on Smokey, roaring down the road that led to the trailer park. As soon as she got within shouting distance, she stretched out both arms and yelled, "Look, Ma, no hands!" Poor Mother nearly fainted.

There were accidents. Like the kick that left a horseshoe outline embedded on my daughter's upper thigh that is there to this day. Or the broken breastbone that put her in the hospital. "Oh, by the way, Tina complained of a sore throat; those tonsils should come out." So, we had that done at the same time. Thursday's dismissal instructions were "Keep her quiet." Saturday I caught her swimming in the river.

Also, there were times when this horse business really got to me. Like when Smokey needed shoes, and I needed shoes. Guess who won? And when Tina and I were having a little heart-to-heart talk. She wished she could have a stallion. So I launched into a vague, low-key talk about the responsibilities of owning a stallion: They weren't docile like Smokey, and (groping) you really had to watch out for them, etc., etc. She turned to me, wide-eyed, and exclaimed, "How did you find out about that?"

After a year of Tina, that once fat, round Smokey was looking considerably less plump. One day, a cowboy from up-country offered a smaller, younger palomino in a trade, explaining that he needed a good mare for breeding. So, for Smokey and another $125, we owned Nugget and a decent saddle, and for another year life continued at its usual breakneck speed.

In June 1959, I was able to unload the business and move 20 miles away to Paradise. Nugget had to be boarded. Tina entered into the horsey group and never lacked for something to do—rides, contests, gymkhanas, you name it. She was always at the stable. My biggest problem was catching up with her.

Inevitably, Mother came to visit again. This time, I had a nice home and was so glad she could see I had survived the Rock House experience and that Tina and I had settled into a fairly well-ordered home life. Now, her only complaint was aimed at Tina and the horse. My soon-to-be husband, Bobby, was having dinner with us when Mother started: "A stable is just no kind of environment for a dainty little girl. Why don't you get rid of that horse and spend the money on piano lessons or something that will help her later in life? Some way she could make money. Good heavens, there's no money in horses."

To which the irrepressible Tina replied, "Oh, no? Do you know how much stud fees are today?"

Poor Bobby. He had just taken a mouthful of steak. When Tina popped off, he choked, and it flew clear across the table. He was so embarrassed, but believe me, not as much as Mother was at the mere mention of stud fees!

Today, Tina, better known as Christina Way, is a more dignified 46-year-old partner in an appraisal business. She never got over her love of horses. I remember she took a week off from riding 20 years ago to have a baby. Now, in addition to my wonderful grandson, she has two beautiful, registered Quarter Horses. She never changed. I hope she never does.

Virginia Tener Bofman died June 5, 1997. Her daughter, Christina, describes her as an "accidental horsewoman," who gave birth to a daughter who was absolutely crazy about horses.

"Mom patiently waited, expecting me to outgrow this passion for horses. Finally, when I was secretly riding after my son was born, she realized that this was probably going to last a lifetime. She supported my love of horses, either by buying them for me when I was very young or by buying them with me when I became an adult." —Christina Way

A Debt Repaid

At first the sickly pony seemed a
dubious investment, but he proved himself to be
a bargain in a blizzard.

SUSAN CASSEL BALDRIGE

The black pony with white socks was just one among 14 ponies milling about in the somewhat rickety barnyard of the horse dealer. But there was something in his personality that drew me to him. There were cuter ponies, and some definitely had had more training. But I loved the way this little fellow went up to a mare with obvious PMS problems and didn't take it personally when she socked him in the gut.

So I bought him. I kept telling myself there had to be a catch. The price was very low, the pony had so much potential, and I could sell him for a terrific profit. It was just too good to be true. Right?

"Is anybody in there?" my husband screamed into my ear less than 48 hours later, as the pony lay somewhat closer to death than to life.

It looked as though I had bought—at a really good price I must mention again—a case of strangles. If you've ever read the rather depressing and maudlin book *The Red Pony*, by John Steinbeck, you're familiar with the disease. Strangles involves a high fever, sneezing and coughing, a rather unsightly discharge, an agonizing death and...well, I don't want to spoil the ending for you.

After examining our prostrate pony and registering his temperature at 104 degrees, our veterinarian had only one tactful piece of advice: "Get him out of here before he infects the whole barn."

That was easier said than done. Oddly, no farm around wanted a highly contagious, near-death pony dragged onto their property. They didn't care how good a buy he was. By the day's end I was down to only one alternative, the 100-year-old structure on our property we affectionately called "the garage." I figured I could slide him in somewhere between the riding mower, the electric hedge trimmers and the dresser I've been refinishing since the late 1970s. But getting him there, two short miles away, was to be another problem entirely.

I roped my friend Pam into helping me trailer him. It was a challenge, to say the least. Have you ever tried to pick up 500 pounds of gelatin? Actually, this pony was limper than gelatin. I might add that the discharge from his nostrils was so nasty that we decided to avoid that area of his body altogether.

"Get in that trailer," I ordered from a safe distance, in my best horse-domination voice, after several attempts to load him had failed. Instead, he sat down like a dog, drooling stringy yellow saliva and gazing at us through glassy eyes.

"We're going to have to sort of lift and push him in," I said.

"Who is?" asked Pam, already looking for a graceful exit upon discovering a suspicious yellow substance stringing along her wrist.

"Come on," I encouraged. "Let's lock our hands behind him and push."

"Lock" was a key word. We roused the pony enough to link hands behind his rump. But like a tree falling in the forest, he couldn't maintain a standing position and collapsed backwards, pinning our hands together on the ground under his weight. By this time, Pam and I were not on friendly terms, certainly not close enough to be holding hands. Our faces were forced together, bright red from a curious mix of exertion and embarrassment. "Let go of my hand," she ordered through gritted teeth. "I can't," I replied, clenching my molars with equal ferocity.

We looked up at our glassy-eyed captor. He looked back at us. Then he inhaled deeply. We were a split second late in realizing what the deep breath meant. What goes in must come out, they say, only this time it was accompanied by a discharge of mucus that showered us with yuck. It was truly amazing how fast we were able to unlock our hands and retreat. It's times like these that are the test of true friendship.

"I'm going home," announced Pam while she tried to wipe big hunks of the discharge off her legs with leaves. "No," I begged her. "Let's try easing him on, little by little." To our relief and surprise, it worked. We put a front foot on the trailer, then we moved a back hoof a little, then a front hoof, then a back hoof. An hour later Gumby was ready for the ride.

It was not difficult getting the pony used to being in a garage since he had the energy level of a bookend. He lay on the deeply bedded wooden floor and groaned between labored breaths. Our veterinarian said the illness would have to run its course without any treatment. Antibiotics, he said, just prolong the symptoms. And just as he predicted, the drainage from the pony's nose ended a week or so later, and the tissue under his jaw began to swell until each gland burst open and drained infection through the skin. We kept him going with hot mashes, aspirin when his fever spiked and lots and lots of tender, loving care. My son, Jordan, and I took shifts soaking his jaw with hot, moist rags three times daily. When he had the energy, we took him for short walks around the yard.

Then, rather suddenly, an eruption the size of a baseball

appeared below the pony's jaw, and his fever shot up to 103 degrees. "I think he's going to die," I told the veterinarian on one of my almost-nightly telephone calls. "No, it's just a large pocket of infection that will burst and drain," he assured me. I briefly pondered bringing the pony into my kitchen that night as temperatures dipped into the low teens. But my husband abruptly ended the pondering by menacingly opening a can of dog food.

Luckily, that was the last gland to drain. In a few days the pony's fever was down and he was contentedly munching hay and sneaking into plastic storage containers for dog biscuits. I knew he was getting better when he began to play with the beach toys each night. But when I caught him getting sleds down, it was past time to return him to the barn. Unfortunately, from all the treks outside in the freezing weather, by then I had a bad case of pneumonia.

Over the next several weeks, Jordan started to ride the pony lightly with a halter and lead rope, and I watched them with content-ment, knowing that all the hard work had not been in vain. The pony was a gentle and willing animal, with an enormous sense of humor.

Finally, I myself recovered—just in time for the blizzard of 1993. To those of us who live on the East Coast, the blizzard of '93 is remem-bered as a time of impassable roads, downed phone and electrical lines and endless and often fruitless shoveling. Unfortunately for Pam and me, the blizzard also meant that the owners of the boarding barn where we kept our healthy horses were unable to return from a cruise in the Caribbean.

The situation was grave. No one could get in to feed our horses or, worse, water them. After waiting a day in vain, hoping the weather would clear, I agonized for several hours and decided there was only one thing to do. I would ride the black pony to the barn and take care of the other horses. Don't worry, I'm not too big; sixth graders often mistake me for an underclassman. Nonetheless, the thought of riding two miles through ice, wind and snow seemed as fun as mucking out stalls with a dinner fork.

Anyway, I did it. I should really say the pony did it. When the 50-mile-per-hour winds whipped a wall of snow across an open field, I huddled down into his mane and he kept trudging. When we came to a stretch of frozen road, he kept going, managing to keep his balance and his direction. Marching past snow blowers, falling ice and branches and howling dogs, the pony never took a bad step.

When we finally reached our destination, we couldn't get into the barn because the snow had drifted higher than my head over the gate. I took a bucket and tunneled through enough for us to squeeze in, and I fed and watered the horses. Then I made the biggest, fluffiest pile of shavings I could, found some choice hay and bedded down my little soldier in his very own stall, one he didn't have to share with leaf rakes and garden hoses. He acted as if it had been nothing and seemed rarin' to go another few miles.

Don't ask me how I got back—that's another story. But I will say that the pony won a place in our hearts that day. And even though I planned to sell him, I decided he needed more work and polish before he was marketed. He willingly learned all his lessons and then taught our daughter to ride in the same year. She fell in love with him, and with that his fate was sealed. We gave him to her for Christmas. He is now considered another family member, with a birthday and a name, Roosevelt, and a lot of special attention.

In his first full year of showing, the black pony won 55 ribbons and six championships and has continued to astound and amaze us with his gentleness, his hard work and, most of all, his ability to make us believe in him.

The Terror Of The Pasture

Taming the Saddlebred
with the notorious reputation required no more than
understanding and apples.

S. LENORE DICKINSON

He stood tall and proud above his small band of mares and assorted geldings. His regal bearing seemed out of place, and yet at home, in that shabby little pasture. He somehow managed to embody all that was good and wild and free in that place bordered by a junior high school, a high school football field and a newer subdivision. I can still close my eyes and see him. I can hear the whispers about how we had to hurry across the pasture through the morning fog in order to avoid getting charged. There is so much about him I remember, and even more that I still miss.

His registered name was Bourbon's Rock and Roll (I later nick-named him Squirrel). He was a 16.3-hand, 1,400-pound, all muscled and sleek chestnut American Saddlebred with two perfectly matched hind stockings. In that year, we were both 12 years of age. I was a tall, overweight adolescent, unsure whether to step out of childhood or remain behind. He was an enormous proud-cut gelding with a small blaze, who was never unsure of anything. He had killed a drunk who tried to beat him, cleanly splitting the man's skull open when backed into a corner. Everyone was afraid of him, including the people in the subdivision, whom he had terrorized one summer afternoon. Why had he not been destroyed? I still don't know, but I like to think that whatever powers govern our lives had kept him safe for me.

There was a small group of us who walked from our own newly formed subdivision, about a mile from the pasture, to our school. One of the members of our group pastured her mare with him and was thus all knowledgeable about his notorious past and vicious nature. She told us we could waste no time taking the shortcut across the pasture and encouraged all of us to dodge between the fallen logs and large boulders in order to keep from "being killed." He was impressive, charging anyone who dared to throw stones or in any way challenge his vast superiority and dominance. I was fascinated and just a little in love.

The boarding situation at the pasture was crude at best, and the girl who had a mare there had to take feed to her equine charge each evening. Being head over heels about horses in general, I asked if I could tag along. She thought it would be a good idea, as I could help her try to chase the gelding away. She explained that he had been all but abandoned and was never fed. His slightly portly appearance at that time was due to the fact that he was "king" of the pasture and commandeered the other horses' food.

On impulse I took several apples the first time I went to help. I had quartered them and taken out all the seeds. As we approached the pasture, I went ahead to check on his location. I found him at his usual place on the upper slope of the pasture, calmly munching the sweet clover that grew there. As I walked toward him, he stopped grazing, raised his head and looked me over. His eyes seemed to stare into my soul. I stopped and somewhat hesitantly pulled an apple out of my pocket, held it up where he could see it, then placed it on the ground. I quietly backed away. He nonchalantly wandered over to the apple and ate it. I was thrilled. He regarded me once more with his questioning eyes. He seemed to ask all at once: "Who are you?" "What do you want?" and "Why?" I pulled out another apple quarter and stepped forward with it. He didn't come forward, but he didn't back away; he just stood there and waited for me, almost like an ancient priest awaiting a sacrifice. I stopped and hesitantly extended my hand with the apple in it. He sniffed at me and, finding nothing to his dislike, serenely took the apple. I took out another piece, and, once again, my offering was accepted. This ritual continued until I had exhausted my supply of apples. He then went back to grazing, but he didn't turn away. I just stood and watched him until the September sun started to set.

I left the pasture with the girl, who thought I had lost my mind. She did, however, ask me if I'd like to help her every day as that had been the first time she hadn't lost her mare's food to him. The next morning on the way to school, she told everyone of my great deed. They all agreed that I was either very brave or very stupid. I let everyone run ahead of me to school and lagged behind, hoping to catch his eye. When I did, he flicked his ears in my direction. I was delighted.

Every morning I would take the big horse apples or carrots, and every afternoon I would buy him more apples from the vending machine at school and offer them to him on my way home. Each evening I accompanied the girl to feed her mare. Within a week, the big horse waited at the gate or the fence bordering my school for my various arrivals. It got to the point that if I was late for school or going home, so was everyone else in our group because no one would walk through the gate or slide through the fence with him standing there. What elation I felt that I could walk through and have him follow me for his daily treats. I soon graduated from simply feeding him to caressing the sleek coat of his neck and talking to him. The day I softly kissed his muzzle and he didn't recoil seemed to be the best day of my life.

One evening as I turned to go home, a black-haired girl on a raw-boned mare loped up and told me that I had best leave him alone, as he would surely turn on me and kill me. She also indicated that the owners wouldn't want me paying any attention to him. I replied that he wouldn't hurt me and that I didn't believe the owners cared at all what happened to him. She shrugged her shoulders and rode away. I walked back up to him, and, even though I no longer had a treat, he allowed me to continue to stroke him. As I turned away a second time, he followed me. Seeing that my friend's mare hadn't finished eating, I climbed up to perch in the roots of one of the fallen trees. He came up and stood beside me, surveying all that belonged to him. It was then that I knew I had been accepted, that I was someone to be trusted and who needn't be watched.

That evening on the walk home, I asked my friend if she knew anything about the gelding's owners. She knew their names and where they lived. The very next Saturday I summoned all my courage and bravado and asked them if I could take care of their horse. I wouldn't charge them anything in exchange for riding privileges. They said I could if I could get my parents to sign a release. I asked my father that afternoon, and, not knowing of the big horse's reputation (I just didn't think to mention it), he signed. I dropped off the release, then ran all the way to the pasture to tell "my" horse the good news.

As his owners had no equipment for him, my wonderful father and I went out and bought a halter, lead rope, several brushes and a bridle. An old cavalry scout saddle was borrowed from a friend of a friend. When Dad found out that the owners didn't feed the gelding, we loaded up two bales of alfalfa and a 50-pound sack of grain into the backseat of my father's company Cadillac. Then I took Dad out to the farm to meet our horse.

The next day when I put the halter and lead rope on the gelding, he reared up, struck out and ran away. The black-haired girl smirked as she said, "See, I told you he'd turn on you." I informed her that I had simply startled him and turned to follow him. As I approached, he shook his head threateningly. I spoke gently to him, reminding him that I was his friend and that I truly loved him. He stopped his aggressive behavior, lowered his head and walked over to me. This time when I slipped my hand around the lead rope, he allowed me to hold it. For several days, I would simply put on the halter and rope and follow him wherever he wanted to go. Gradually, he allowed me to lead him.

When I first put the borrowed saddle on the gelding's back, no small feat in itself, he bucked and threw it on the ground, eyeing me suspiciously. I then showed the saddle and blanket to him and next tried to saddle him as I fed him. This time, he allowed me my small victory. Over the next several days, he allowed me to continue to saddle him, then bridle him and then lead him around. I announced to the black-haired girl that on the next Saturday I would ride him.

Saturday morning dawned bright and crisp. When I got to the stable, everyone was waiting to watch me get dumped and stomped into the earth. They had managed to pen him up in the small corral at one end of the pasture, and he was fast becoming more than a little annoyed. When I spoke to him, he walked toward the fence and affectionately greeted me.

I followed our usual routine of treats, brushing and saddling. As I climbed up into the saddle, he tensed, humping his back. As I sat down, he turned around, realized it was me and lovingly nuzzled my leg, totally relaxing. Comparatively, the smile on my face was as large as the look of astonishment on the faces of my fellow boarders. I trotted him around the corral and then asked someone to open the gate. I spent the entire day riding. It was heaven.

That Thanksgiving my parents purchased Squirrel and gave him to me for Christmas. Over the next 10 years, we were inseparable, and he took care of me. Anyone who yelled at me or did anything he considered in any way threatening or upsetting was summarily charged and driven off.

He taught me many things, and not just those having to do with riding skills. Because of him I became a skilled, powerful and aggressive rider. He taught me love, patience and a selflessness I shall never forget. I believe he had almost as much influence on me as my parents, and certainly more than any other being ever had or ever will.

When Squirrel was 22, he developed cancer, and I had to decide if he should be put down. I knew he was dying, and I also knew that I had only one choice: to help him die with dignity and pride. The veterinarian told me to leave the stable and he would see it done. I couldn't do that. Squirrel had been with me through all those years, never once letting me down, never once letting me go through anything alone. I cradled his head in my arms as the veterinarian gave him the lethal injection. The night he died was the first time I ever saw my father cry. Even though I knew my parents and best friend were there beside me, I never felt so alone in all my life. I felt Squirrel had gone and taken the best part of me with him.

Six months later, however, it occurred to me that I really wanted and needed another horse. I was backed into going to see a beautiful but unbroke, rank, sour and thoroughly nasty bay Arabian-Saddlebred gelding. I bought him that night. My friends know I bought him because of his nature, not in spite of it. We've been together for close to eight years now; he's developed into a truly outstanding Class A show horse, and this year we head for the Canadian nationals. Somehow I know Squirrel would approve.

My Running Quarter Horse

*A little Thoroughbred blood makes
one trail mount a racetrack contender.*

CATHERINE PICKERING

A little better than two years ago, I admitted—with some reluctance—
that it was time to retire Charlie, my Arabian-Morgan pleasure horse of
15 years. At that time, Charlie was in his 20s, and he had provided me
with many good times and fond memories. So in gratitude for the
countless hours we'd spent together on the trail, I wished only to grant
him the richest and happiest of retirements and to ensure (for my own
selfish love of him) that he would be gracing our pastures for many
years to come.

Of course, this meant I would need a new horse, and that, in
turn, meant the challenge of finding a suitable mount. I had decided I
wanted a ready-made, saddle-and-serve, pleasure and trail horse—one
who was also extra-large and extra-sound, as I am, by no means, "a
little slip of a girl."

By a stroke of luck, very shortly into my search, I found a big,
red, stocky Quarter Horse named Tex, who had been born deep in the
heart of the Lone Star State and had been hauled up north to Michigan
for sale as an A-1 pleasure horse. Tex had run cattle all of his life and
was described to me as a good all-around ranch horse, as dependable

and easygoing as they come. He wasn't an especially impressive or expensive animal, but having found him to be large, muscular, sound and healthy—with documentation of the full battery of tests and immunizations required to cross many state lines—I purchased him without asking too many questions.

Many weeks later, when Tex's transfer of registration came through, I noticed a "TB" listed after his sire's name on the pedigree. When I casually asked my older sister, Mary, what this meant, she replied, "You know what that is. It means Tex is half-Thoroughbred. His sire was a Thoroughbred."

"Hmmm...neat," I responded, pausing to ponder this information. My new horse was a tad more interesting than I previously had thought. Then I filed the papers away and put the whole thing out of my mind.

The next two years passed somewhat uneventfully. I spent many hours just quietly enjoying my delightful and good-natured horse. He carried me over many miles of trail and also every once in a while enthusiastically took part in the monthly gymkhana events our local riding club conducts. On a couple of occasions, my sister took Tex out in an open field nearby and ran him for all he was worth. Their speed seemed dizzying, and yet for Tex it was effortless. After one of these workouts, when my sister finally reined Tex around and pulled him to a halt, she proclaimed in an exhausted breath as she slid to the ground, "This is the fastest horse I have ever ridden. He's got to be the fastest horse in the county!"

"Yeah, right," was my reply as I took the reins from her and turned to walk Tex home. As I unsaddled him and rubbed him down, I noticed that despite the all-out effort, his breathing had quickly returned to normal and his skin was only slightly damp. It didn't seem to have phased him at all. I was aware that good feed and regular evening and weekend outings were keeping him in tip-top shape, but still, many horses stay wound up for a long period after a gallop like that. Shrugging my shoulders, I put Tex to bed with a scoop of sweet feed, a flake of hay and a good-night kiss but still gave no serious thought to his breeding or his speed.

Amateur Rodeo Day is a big event in our county, held the first Sunday of August every year in front of the fairgrounds grandstand. It is sponsored by our local riding club and has kicked off the county fair for 25 years. This year, my farrier, who is also a very fine trainer and horseman, asked to borrow my Texas-bred horse to compete in a couple events. He has a special fondness for Tex, and Tex for him, so I thought they would make a good team. I had my horse saddled, bridled, shined up and fit as a fiddle for Ray on Rodeo Sunday.

They had a lot of fun that day and made a couple of good showings in their events, but the last and most grueling contest was a four-member relay race. I was holding Tex as Ray prepared for the event, putting on the T-shirt that matched those worn by his three other teammates. When they gathered to map out their strategy, I was surprised to hear Ray say, "It doesn't matter what positions we take, we aren't going to win anyway."

I couldn't hold my tongue. With wounded pride, I looked over the tall, elegant, copper-colored mass of equine muscle next to me and told Ray firmly, "You run this horse dead last and you'll win!"

He stared at me silently for a few minutes before he answered, "Well…all right."

Snatching Tex's reins from me, he swung aboard and rode off. I was pretty sure I'd just put my foot in my mouth. I had no true measure of my horse's speed or ability, just Mary's word, and we'd soon see what that was worth.

Now relay races can be confusing to watch—some teams being

wildly fast-paced, others having trouble handing off the baton, and still others losing control and falling off their horses. From my vantage point atop my pickup cab in the infield, I tried in vain to figure out which team was in the lead. Eventually, I gave up and focused my attention on my beautiful horse, standing and waiting contentedly at the far turn. In contrast, his opponents tugged furiously against the death grips of their riders as they waited for the baton to come around the track.

The third horse of team number one came speeding into view. The rider handed off the baton, and his teammate sped away. Like clockwork, then came the second team, followed by the third. Still Tex stood waiting, not understanding but fully aware that he had not been given the command to go. A little bay mare, running her heart out, sidled right up alongside Tex as he began cantering, and the handoff to Ray was effortless. Still, my heart sank. No matter how smooth the handoff was, the other horses were already a good quarter mile ahead of Tex in the half-mile stretch to the finish.

But then something magical happened. My big beautiful brute of a horse stuck his neck out and drove his haunches down. With ground-eating strides that would have rivaled those of Man o' War, Tex devoured the track. In seconds he was on the heels of the other horses. Gliding and weaving through the tightly knit group, he burst ahead and finished first by a very generous and effortless margin.

I heard myself and my sister shrieking with joy. My horse had given no harried or wild-eyed desperate chase but had, instead, glided like a speed skater past the pack and forward toward the finish line. Then I heard the grumblings of some skeptics in the infield who surmised that Tex had won only because the very best team had a fallen rider. Not being a race or speed expert by any means, I did not offer a rebuttal. I simply came back down to earth and dashed off to tend to the needs of my hardworking horse.

"Perhaps those railbirds are right," I thought to myself as I jogged toward Ray and Tex. "Maybe this was just dumb luck." But now, at least, the wheels of wonder were turning.

I lay awake that night, contemplating what Tex might do on his own merit. I tried hard to picture again the blazing speed my sister had gotten out of him. I never let him run full-out myself, fearing that doing so too often would ruin my nice pleasure horse. Still, what could Tex do on his own? What if he were put on the track fresh, alert and hungry, up against some truly worthy adversaries? What if this horse, in a lifetime invested in cow punching and trail blazing, had somewhere flowing in his veins three centuries of select, royal racing blood that would allow him to drive down a racetrack in first place?

"Naaahhh!" I rolled over and drifted off to sleep, putting such thoughts out of my mind.

Ironically, the next day the phone rang, and catching me quite off guard, the young man on the other end asked, "Would you like someone to race your horse in the quarter mile on Wednesday? I saw him race on Sunday. Ray told me that he can't be there that afternoon and that maybe you'd need a rider."

I had forgotten all about the races, but I was intrigued by the idea of entering Tex. I knew that Scott, the young man now on the phone, had the reputation of being a hearty, fast and fearless horseman. I knew he could handle Tex and get the best out of him. On a whim, I agreed, and at 3:30 p.m. on Wednesday, I had my horse at the fairgrounds, fresh, alert and hungry.

Spotting us soon after our arrival, my "jockey" approached my sister and me with a smile, then climbed aboard and gave Tex a whirl out in the large field adjacent to the fairgrounds, hoping to gauge his speed and ability before race time. Well, Tex didn't know that speed was what this guy was looking for, so he simply gave his best, collected, easygoing, cattle-cutting pace. He was quick on the turn, making tight figure eights, stopping on a dime and wheeling around at the slightest touch of the rein. The boy brought my horse back with what I noticed was an obvious look of disappointment. I didn't know how to tell him that this horse had speed if he would seriously ask for it. But before I could get the words out, Scott excused himself, saying he had other horses to warm up for the other races of the day. Jogging away, he turned and shouted over his shoulder, "Just have him ready for me when the quarter mile is called."

I patted Tex as he stood dozing in the shade of the trailer. Had I made a big mistake by bringing him here?

All too soon, it was quarter-mile time, and I hadn't had a chance to take Scott aside and explain the technique and ability that my humble-looking horse truly possessed. I could only hope now that he would somehow get the feel for Tex's big stride once he was in the group and well away. I led Tex onto the track and into the infield to hand him over to the jockey. As I looked back over my shoulder, filing onto the track one-by-one came what I knew to be a collection of the very fastest quarter-mile horses in the county. With my heart in my throat, I now prayed that Tex wouldn't come in dead last. I had seen all of these horses race—and win—on several occasions. I looked at my snoozing horse. Had I truly expected that unassuming little "TB" on his pedigree to fuel him past these horses?

Wordlessly, Scott swung up onto Tex's back and whisked him away. I ran to the grandstand to be with my sister and a few of our friends who had gathered to help us cheer Tex on. Across the track, I could see the other horses on their way to the starting line, dancing and prancing, full of themselves and hard to contain. My cow pony jogged along like an old gentleman. His rider, I was certain, must have been thinking that he had made a big mistake by offering us his services.

Worse yet, Tex had drawn the outside position, putting him in the most difficult spot on the track, having to run along the outside of five other horses. Many quarter-mile races are run on the straightaway, but at our little community fairgrounds, the quarter-mile mark begins at the far turn. My horse would have to race 75 percent of the contest on this turn.

Suddenly, my dark and foreboding thoughts were interrupted by "AND THEY'RE OFF!" All the horses lunged forward with one great collective leap, but there behind them, starting at an easygoing canter, was Tex. His rider, sitting back and riding with one hand, did not seem the least bit interested in urging him on in any way. My face grew hot with anger. I stood and shouted, "Race my horse! Race him!"

And then—just as in the relay race three days earlier—something happened. Suddenly, those three centuries of race breeding were urging my horse on. With his tremendous ground-eating strides, Tex began to career around the tightly knit bunch running on the rail. He was way to the outside, but undaunted. Stretched flat-out and pummeling the earth, my tall, sleek, fiery red bullet finally convinced his rider that he was indeed sitting on a contender. To my delight, Scott took the reins in both hands and crouched low over Tex's withers.

As they headed into the homestretch, a couple of horses shot out ahead, but Scott gave a war whoop, and Tex surged forward alongside them. Running neck and neck with the leader, and with only a few yards to the finish, Tex gave one last burst and a fully extended leap and it was all over. He won by a full head and shoulder!

The crowd roared with excitement. I was hysterical, but I never took my eyes off Tex. I watched as the other horses continued to run around the track, their riders pulling back ferociously in an effort to stop them. But Tex's jockey gave one pull on the reins, and my horse slid to a halt. This maneuver catapulted Scott up between Tex's ears, but, there was no harm done—the boy quickly scrambled down onto his mount's back and breezed around the track to cool him.

After being congratulated by my friends and a few of the folks in the stands, my sister and I sauntered to the infield to gather Tex up and be on our way. Scott spotted me and came forward, leading my lithe and handsome horse, who already had regained his composure. Then he handed over the reins, and with his face beaming, he thanked me. "Boy, this horse runs funny," he added breathlessly. "But that was fun. It's been a long time since I was in the winner's circle."

"Runs funny…?" I thought to myself, "Child, that's called fast!" Tex had been clocked at 20 seconds flat.

As we all headed back toward the stable, the riders and owners of the losing horses ribbed me good-naturedly about how Tex had taken them all by surprise, just like the proverbial dark horse of old.

"Dark horse, indeed," I whispered under my breath to Tex as we walked toward our trailer. "You were the one horse here today bred on both sides for nothing but blazing speed."

Tex gave me a very hard nudge as if to say, "Don't go soft in the head now, girl, and don't get any bright ideas. Let's just go home and have some oats. My racing career started and finished right here in one day."

It was just a friendly, county-fair race among some of the faster horses in the neighborhood, and no one is any richer for its running. But my adversaries are already busy bringing up and training the horses they think will pass Tex next time. He apparently set a standard that many area horsemen are determined to match or surpass, and I truly wish them all good luck in their endeavors. But Tex won't be giving them a chance to redeem themselves against him. At 13 years of age, he now has a much nobler pursuit: to continue to be the one horse on earth that could possibly replace an irreplaceable trail horse.

The Convert

*An ancient mare teaches
a doubting parent the true definition of "perfection."*

CHRISTINE WILLARD

Unlike most horse owners, I got dragged into buying a horse. I had no dreamy fantasies of flowing manes and thundering hooves. I had never even read *Misty of Chincoteague*. I was thrust into it by my horse-crazy daughter, but I must admit now that owning a horse has transformed both of our lives.

Nicole was crazy about horses from the first time she saw one, when she was a year old. After that, her favorite toys were horses; she had a bouncy horse in the kitchen, and her favorite television show was a *National Geographic* special on Irish horses.

Each of those I found to be manageable, but as Nicole grew, she wanted the real thing. When she was eight, we moved from the suburbs to a more rural area. I decided I could take the next step for my daughter. We got some local recommendations, and Nicole started taking lessons. The trainer she began with was a dressage rider, not really the best match for a romantic young girl who wanted the wind in her hair, but Nicole was thrilled at just being allowed to ride a horse, and she began to master the basics. I sat on the sidelines and did my part: paying for the lessons and cheering her on.

This girl lived for horses, and she began to spend more and more time hanging out at the ranch, doing odd jobs and hoping for occasional rides. I was beginning to realize that she would have to have her own horse one of these days. "When you're a teenager," I told her. That time seemed far enough off that I could think of a diversion between now and then.

What I didn't take into account was the speed with which events can gallop up and overtake you. One day someone mentioned a small mare that might be for sale at the next ranch over. Confident of my ability to find some reason why any horse would be unacceptable, I allowed myself to be persuaded to go see her.

A dirty chestnut horse stood quietly in one of the run-down corrals. She turned to look at us when we came to her gate, hardly even responding to our presence. A young roan mare corralled with her made some nervous moves, putting herself between us and the chestnut.

The cowboy who ran the ranch explained that he'd actually wanted only the roan horse, but the chestnut came along as part of the deal. Both horses had belonged to an old cowboy who'd died a couple of years ago. No one had done anything about the horses, and the two had lived on the acreage since then, fending for themselves.

They certainly looked it with their scruffy coats. Suspicious and unfriendly, the chestnut mare was so far from the ideal pony that it would be easy to put off the decision again.

"She's real gentle," he told us, entering the corral. The roan snorted nervously and began a skittish dance, so he led the chestnut out the back of the corral, closing a rickety old gate between the two horses. "Here, look, nothing bothers her," he said, grabbing her tail and leaning back, letting it hold him up. She took a step and gave him an annoyed look, then turned away. I watched this spectacle with a mixture of horror and relief: Even after such an extreme demonstration of her gentleness, I was sure my daughter wouldn't want this creature that barely resembled a horse.

"Here, she can sit on her," the cowboy went on, lifting an eager Nicole onto the horse's back. Holding onto the lead rope, she let the horse take a few steps. Suddenly, with a snort and a crash, the barricaded young roan came thundering through the rickety gate, determined to reclaim her companion. She charged directly toward my daughter and the older mare.

The chestnut looked over her shoulder at the commotion, laid her ears back and stood her ground. The roan eventually settled at the chestnut's side, until the cowboy haltered the younger horse and led her away. The chestnut stayed steady through it all, my daughter secure on her back. Nicole began to walk the horse around the corral. I was relieved that disaster hadn't overtaken us and grateful that the old mare had not taken the separation from her buddy as seriously as the roan. But Nicole saw a dream coming true.

"I love her, Mom. Can we get her? Please, please?"

"Well, we'll see. She's very nice. What a good old girl." I would say anything to get out of this.

But something had changed for me. I realized that I had committed myself to getting Nicole a horse. No turning back now. I was terrified of acquiring this one, though, because she was a mess. I had no experience with horses. What kind of potential problems was she harboring, and how would we know how to deal with them? What we needed was a pony all set up, ready to go. Nicole grudgingly said she'd look at other ponies but swore that she loved this one. I felt sure that we would find some other horse that she would love even more, something we could manage.

We traveled around and tried out other horses and ponies. We met Tony the Pony, who'd won jumping classes and presented a sharp, ideal pony appearance. His teenage owner showed him well. Surely this was the answer. We arranged for him to come out for a lesson. Although Nicole still insisted she wanted only the old mare, I felt certain she'd come around and fall in love with Tony.

Every day we passed the old mare on our way to the ranch. We'd bring her small treats and visit with her. One day I brought an apple. Perhaps she hadn't tasted an apple in years, but for the first time I saw a light come on behind her eyes as she ate it. Carefully taking each piece from my hand, she showed me some sparkle. Her grateful old eye took on a younger look. "Why, I hardly remember ever having anything so delicious, dear," she seemed to say. She really was a gentle old girl, a honey of a pony.

We asked a friend to ride her. The mare had all her gaits and was a willing and honest horse, the friend pronounced. What does "honest" mean, applied to a horse, I asked. Well, she does what you ask as well as she can, our friend explained. That sounded positive.

Perhaps the veterinarian would save me from winding up with the old mare. We had him out, a kind, youngish man in whom I'd developed confidence as I watched him work with horses at the ranch. Surely he'd find this ancient critter unsuitable and free us to find the Perfect Pony.

No help from him. He pronounced her sound and healthy—thin and dirty, with some paddling in her gait, but nothing to keep us from using this horse for a girl's first pony. He found her to be much older than the 15 years the cowboy had claimed was her age, probably more than 25. Too old, I said, adding that to my list of objections.

Yet something inside me was slipping. "At least give Tony a chance," I told a pleading Nicole. "Try him for the lesson Monday."

But Sunday afternoon Tony's owner called. A nice family had

come to see the pony and had bought him, she told me. No lesson tomorrow; sale canceled. I regrouped for a minute and finally looked the future straight in the eye. "Well, I guess you can get the old mare," I heard myself tell Nicole. She whooped with joy.

After dickering with the cowboy over price, we walked the mare, whom we named Honey, up the hill to her new home. Nicole was thrilled, but I still had my doubts. What would we do with her? What did either of us know about owning a horse? Fortunately, the dressage barn provided full board—albeit at a price, both in dollars and in sneers. But it gave us time to learn what feed was best for her, what farrier we trusted to trim her feet and the basics of horse care. Soon we were ready to move her to a self-care ranch where we'd all be happier.

From that first day, when keeping Nicole on her back was more important than indulging her companion's antics, Honey seemed to take real pride in protecting my daughter. Somewhere in her past, perhaps, she had once had another young girl of her own whom she'd trained to be a responsible horsewoman.

Honey seemed to take personally any insufficiency on her rider's part as an area she'd have to work on training. Nicole was fortunate to have good natural balance, and Honey turned out to be a trustworthy companion on whom my daughter could learn to ride as well as grow up. The two of them cantered across the fields together, rode to the beach, rode trails into the hills. Having her own horse legitimized Nicole as a serious rider at the ranch. No more begging rides and hoping for the best. Now she worked on mastering skills in earnest.

Eventually, Honey took her to local horse shows, and Nicole covered a wall of her room with ribbons. She took up sidesaddle riding and won a trophy in a parade. Presently, they are learning to drive in harness. If Nicole wants to try something, Honey does her best, which often is very good and rarely less than respectable.

As for myself, a bookish type who thought having a second cup of tea was an eventful afternoon, I've changed my life completely. Now we are outdoors in the fresh air, working and playing hard every day, with Honey, our faithful companion and teacher. I never tire of her patient company, and, in return, I take great pride in keeping Honey looking nice.

The entire focus of our lives has changed. Even at the very start, Honey's patience and devotion transformed us. She continues to lead us to greater humanity with every fulfilling day. I've never regretted for a moment that quiet evening when I agreed to buy this Perfect Pony.

A member of the hunter/jumper community, Christine Willard has been involved with horses for six years and has found time to work with horse rescue organizations near her home in Los Osos, California.

"Honey came to live with us in 1991. Over the years, she suffered from recurrent uveitis and glaucoma. In late 1996, her vision flickered out.

"We struggled to help her while she raged in fear and confusion. Eventually, she gained confidence and learned to cope in a dark world. One day a new boarder asked about Honey's milky eyes, and I launched into an abridged version of her troubles. The woman looked at Honey and reached out a hand to pet her. 'Oh,' she said, 'I thought it made her look like a wise, magical horse.'" —Christine Willard

CHAPTER 2

Through Thick and Through Thin

The Odd Couple

*How the heroic rescue of a starving old pony
saved an angry ex-racehorse's life.*

BOBBYE S. WICKE

Avoiding the house trailer meant an extra 10 miles backtracking, so I drove past it whenever we had an errand in the city. I stepped on the gas as we approached it, agreed with the children's expressions of outrage and tried not to look at the pony.

Once, driving alone, I stopped at the trailer. There were no signs of life, not even from the animal tied in the yard, but I picked my way around the debris in my path and knocked on the door. I stood on the metal stoop for several minutes, feeling foolish and vulnerable miles from any friendly eyes, and listened to movement inside the trailer. Another tentative rap on the door caused it to be opened a few inches by a huge woman. Big eyes in pale faces peered around her, like mushrooms sprouting from a mother mountain, and odors of burnt grease and unwashed diapers wafted through the crack in the door.

"I'm sorry to bother you," I said. "Is that your pony?"

"Yeah. Why?"

"I wondered if you would like to sell it."

"No," she said, "the kids like it," and she closed the door.

Well, I had tried. I should be relieved that I hadn't bought an obviously diseased and worthless animal, or been bitten by a pit bull. No dog, I realized; we could just come take it away. An enticing idea. I resolved to take the long way to town in the future and to forget the shaggy little bag of bones chained to a stake in the burning, shadeless sand.

Months later, hurrying to a dental appointment in the city, I took the shortcut past the trailer again. When it was too late to turn back, the children remembered and began to look for the pony. There he stood, with all four feet braced wide apart. His nose almost touched the sand, his eyes stared from deep sockets at an overturned water bucket, and his ears pricked hopefully forward. Great clumps of the shaggy coat had fallen away, leaving raw, red patches of bare skin stretched over a gaunt frame. Sickened, I took my foot off the gas pedal, and the car coasted to a stop. The middle child began to bawl in sympathy with the furious comments of the other children, and I stepped on the gas again and sped on, feeling ashamed and somehow responsible.

"Mom, we have to do something."

"I tried," I replied. "I called the Humane Society. I called the newspapers and the police. I even stopped by there one day and tried to buy the pony."

"They ought to be put in jail!"

"You're right. I just don't know what we can do about it. Please stop crying, Mary. The dentist will think I beat you."

"We ought to just go get it one night," my son suggested. That brought enthusiastic cheers, and the children began to plan the horse theft of the century. In the dentist's parking lot, I broke into the furor, "Sounds good. But then I would be put in jail," saying the words, not believing them. To continue to do nothing was the crime.

"No one would know he was at the farm," said Janie, the logical child. "You can't see the farm from the road and the gate is locked."

"Stealing is a crime," I said firmly.

We planned it over dinner that night. The two youngest children would go to bed early, to be awakened at midnight and taken along. We thought the full moon would be perfect.

Sounds of the late movie came through the curtained windows of the trailer, and a truck parked in the yard partially shielded the occupants from a view of the pony. He made no sound or movement as I unsnapped his halter from the chain, but he dug his heels firmly into the sand when I urged him forward. Taking his tail in one hand and his halter in the other, I dragged him to the shelter of the brush beside the road, where the children waited. His incredible lightness gave me an eerie sensation of handling something fragile and unreal.

It was a long mile, even when the pony began to walk slowly on his own and we no longer had to push and drag him along, because we could be seen for a mile in the bright moonlight. We panicked at the sound of an approaching car. No one else lived on the road—they must have called the sheriff. We pushed the pony into the brush and huddled ankle deep in stagnant ditch water, too scared to feel the bites of hundreds of hungry mosquitoes while we hid our prize from the passing headlights of an ordinary passenger car.

When we let ourselves through the gate into our own safe pasture, we were shaking from the damp chill, the excitement and the fear; one of the younger children was coughing and another crying from mosquito bites. The pony's steps quickened then, as the wind from the bay blew the smell of our horses to him, and they nickered softly to the newcomer, giving us new reason to fear we would be heard and discovered. We hustled the pony into the stall that we had freshly bedded for him and waited for the sounds of pursuit. When the night noises of the woods and swamp resumed, we turned on the lights to examine our booty.

In the bright light, the pony stood as if nailed to the ground, staring, with his ears still pricked hopefully forward. He was incredibly thin, greasily filthy and unresponsive to offers of food and water. We were baffled by his lack of response until we saw that he turned his head toward the voice of the speaker. Janie, the oldest, waved her fingers at his eyes.

"I don't believe this, Mom," she said. "Six people stealing a blind, starved, half-dead old white pony on a moonlit night." She began to laugh, and we joined her in hysterical relief.

"Maybe it's night blindness?"

"Why won't he eat?"

"What are we going to do? We won't be able to let him out!"

"He'll fall in the canal and drown!" Mary began to cry again.

"We're going to think about it in the morning," I said. "Right now, in case he really is blind, I'm going to show him where the walls are and park him in front of the hay and water." I took his halter and tail again to lead him around the stall, and touched his nose to each wall and then into the water bucket and the hay before we left him.

In the sober light of morning, the pony stood right where we had left him, with a little pile of hard, dry manure pellets behind him and the untouched hay and water at his head. A few wisps of hay floated forlornly on the water. We made a hot bran mash and pushed it into his mouth with our fingers. He opened his mouth just enough to let the feed fall to the ground.

"We're probably going to have to have him put down," I said, thinking I'd better get the idea across before anyone got attached to this pathetic little creature.

"Gee, Mom," John said, "first kidnapping and now murder."

"The worst part," retorted the logical child, "is five counts of contributing to the delinquency of a minor!" She poked the manure pellets with her toe. "Look, one system is working. He's not quite dead. We ought to at least give him a chance."

"Maybe he's just scared," offered the littlest daughter.

"Tell you what," I said, "we'll have the vet check him over and see if he's got enough liver and heart left to enjoy life for a little while—if we can save him. Don't get your hopes up, though. His mucous membranes are yellow, and he nearly falls down when we make him move. We could put in a lot of work, get attached to him, and still have to have him destroyed."

Blood tests indicated that about five percent of the pony's liver was functioning, and the veterinarian found him irreversibly blind, both conditions resulting from prolonged starvation. He would not eat now, simply because he had forgotten how and because he had lost the instinct to fight to live. To the vet's amused quip that he thought he'd seen this pony somewhere, I replied, nonchalantly, that "we have all seen this pony everywhere."

The children worked on the old pony for weeks, organizing themselves around a schedule of forced feeding—putting feed in his mouth and trying to make him swallow—and forced exercise—dragging him about the stall in the hope that using his muscles would stim-ulate his appetite. They picked the snarls and knots out of the filthy mane and tail and found a pink plastic curler buried deep in his mane, perhaps left by another child who had loved him once. We couldn't agree on a name for something more dead than alive, and he became "The Old Man." The veterinarian warned that we would likely find him dead in his stall one morning, and it became routine to ask the doer of morning chores, "Did The Old Man make it through the night?"

To lessen the risk of infectious disease to the other horses, The Old Man was kept in an end stall where his only neighbor was a handsome and expendable Thoroughbred gelding known as Cappy.

Cappy's career at the racetrack had outlasted his knees: At six he was the trainer's darling, always sore-kneed and angry at the world but sure to win in the right class and distance. At eight years old, he was discarded because he absolutely refused to run anymore.

Cappy had responded to our attempts to retrain him with alternate disdain and fury. Sometimes he refused to move at all, displaying a great deal more patience than his two-legged mentors. When I walked and trotted him, Cappy went along pleasantly for a little while, flicking his ears back and forth at me. If I relaxed and let him canter, he stopped on a dime, put his head down and deposited me at his front feet. He spared me his favorite evasion: bolting and running madly in whatever direction he was pointed until he was too winded to take another step. That dangerous habit had earned him the retirement he wanted, at least temporarily. But we weren't in the retirement-home business, and a big healthy Thoroughbred gelding consumes his own weight in feed about every 90 days. If we could rehabilitate him, his good looks would ensure a sale and a successful career; if not, he would have to be destroyed.

Cappy was fascinated by his new neighbor and tried all the tricks he knew to get into the stall with him. In light of Cappy's past benevolence toward man and horse, we assumed he merely wanted to murder the pony. The Old Man paid no attention to Cappy's nickering and hanging over his stall door, or to anything else for a long time.

After many weeks, something in The Old Man's metabolism, or maybe in his soul, began to smolder, and he swallowed a little more feed each day. Hair began to grow on the red patches of skin; the coarse, greasy fur fell away and a new silvery-gray coat emerged. He began to walk—slowly, but willingly—when led. After prudently catching and shutting up Cappy each day, the children walked The Old Man out into the sunshine, and the pony turned his blind face up to the sun as if to soak up its warm strength. He began to stroll about his stall, stopping at his door and listening to the barn activities, or stopping at Cappy's wall and provoking him into giving the wall a warning kick.

On a perfect spring day, when The Old Man was taken out for his walk, he danced about and kicked up his little heels in sheer exuberance, as if he were a yearling again. In celebration of the pony's newfound enthusiasm for life, we decided to give him a bath—maybe his first ever, we joked. He stood contentedly for a quick sudsing; then we carried buckets of lukewarm water out to the barnyard to rinse him. Cappy stomped and fretted as he watched us over the half door of his stall, shaking his head, circling the stall and returning to the door to shake his head at us again. As I lifted the first rinse bucket to pour over The Old Man, Cappy became airborne. The horse that had refused to lift his feet to trot over cavalletti popped gracefully over a four-foot stall door and bore down on us with a vengeance.

I dropped the bucket, six people scattered in six directions, and before anyone had time to cry out, "He'll kill The Old Man," Cappy had cut the pony out of our midst and, nose to withers, was rushing The Old Man across the pasture toward the canal. Stunned, we started after them to rescue the pony, spreading out to corner them.

"Wait, Mom," Janie said. "I don't think he's going to hurt him." We stood and watched silently as Cappy stopped the pony near the canal, and they began to graze side by side, their noses almost touching. We exchanged incredulous looks. Cappy was not going to savage the pony. Cappy was not going to let us savage the pony with buckets of water, either. We didn't get the soapy pony back until the next morning, when hunger overcame love and Cappy brought The Old Man up to the barn for the morning feed.

Cappy had a job now, a labor of love. He took The Old Man out to pasture each morning, guided him gently away from fences and canals, and defended him fiercely from other curious horses. They grazed together in the sun, and when the weather turned bad they came into the shelter of the barn together, Cappy adjusting his quick pace to the old pony's slow steps. The Old Man grew plump and shiny, although his faltering steps, yellow mucous membranes and opaque eyes betrayed the fragility of his health. We didn't talk about the two of them much beyond an occasional joke about "the odd couple." We accepted them with wonder and unspoken knowledge of what was to come.

In late winter, The Old Man began to fail. Each day, he ate less, and he required a nap in the sunshine after the short walk out to pasture with Cappy. The Thoroughbred waited patiently while the old pony dozed, and when the days came that The Old Man would not come out of his stall, Cappy would not come out either. We went through token efforts of vitamin shots, feed delicacies and warm blankets, then had the veterinarian out.

"Quite honestly," he said, "his heart's gone, his liver's gone. I don't know what's keeping him on his feet."

I knew what was keeping him on his feet, besides the fact that a dying horse knows that once it's down it's not likely to get up again, and I thought about it for several moments before saying: "Well, we were expecting this, and he's probably had the best year of his life. It's almost spring, though. We'll give him a couple of weeks of nice weather, if he makes it that far without pain, and you can put him down when you come out to do this year's Coggins tests." I didn't mention Cappy, there was nothing to say.

The Old Man rallied briefly in the spring and greeted each new morning of warm sun and gentle breezes with a bright hopeful demeanor for a month, while Cappy hovered anxiously over him. But the old pony still picked tiredly at his feed, still lost weight, and at the end of the month, I called the vet. He and Janie took The Old Man out to his favorite spot and put him to sleep while Cappy stood by his side.

In midsummer, one of Janie's students came to the farm for a dressage lesson. Marcia was a gutsy rider who had made do with horses whose best was somewhat less than hers. Her lesson over, we were having the usual lean-on-the-fence chat while her horse cooled out in the paddock, when she said, "He's really beautiful, isn't he?"

"Thank you, but who?" I asked.

"The bright chestnut over there," she replied, indicating Cappy moping near the barn, which was all he had done for weeks.

"Oh, Cappy," said Janie, disparagingly. "Yeah, he's pretty sporty looking."

"Is something wrong with him?" Marcia asked.

"Yes," I answered. "He hasn't done any work for a year, and if we don't get something done with him before winter comes, I'm going to have to send him to the Great Pasture in the Sky."

"That's terrible," Marcia groaned. "I'd kill for a horse like that."

"He was pretty sour when he came off the track last year," Janie said. "In fact, he was pretty dangerous. We can't even think about selling him right now. He needs more time than I have, and he's not safe for the little kids and Mom."

"I'd love to work with a horse like that," Marcia said, "but I don't think I'll ever be able to afford one."

While she and Janie talked of other things, I regarded Marcia thoughtfully: a small, sturdy, competent girl, as plain as the horses she rode. She put so much into those discarded horses. She got so much out of them, an astonishing percentage of seconds and thirds and fourths with horses that went unnoticed until the points were added up, and unremembered later. We had watched her struggles with mediocre horses for a long time, and we liked her enormously. I tried to sort out whether I was more concerned with a decent solution for Cappy or with a genuine desire to see what Marcia could do with a classy-looking, athletic horse who wasn't afraid of anything except pain, or perhaps with being the cause of a friend's being injured.

I watched her watching Cappy for several minutes, then I said, "Marcia, there are some other reasons we haven't worked with Cappy this year, which don't have anything to do with his problems, and I really would like to see him get a chance. I think he has a lot of ability and heart, and that he's serviceably sound for a good rider—although I wouldn't have said so last year. But Janie's right that he's not safe."

"You remember the last safe horse I had!" Marcia laughed, but the pain in her eyes made us remember the reliable mare that broke down and had to be destroyed just as she'd begun to win with her—the first horse she'd owned, not much bigger than a pony, but kind and willing.

"I'll sell you Cappy for what I paid for him," I said, "if you are interested. On time, however you can afford to pay. But you will have to work with him here first, so I can see that it will work out."

Janie was appalled; Marcia was ecstatic. I was apprehensive and could hardly bring myself to watch Marcia work with Cappy. Back under saddle after his sabbatical, Cappy never took a wrong step. Marcia shone on the flashy Thoroughbred. She took him away a few days later, and in a few months she finished paying for him. In some ways, I guess Cappy was a cheap horse.

We didn't see Marcia and Cappy again until spring returned, when they beat the socks off us at an important competition. Maybe the ghost of The Old Man rode with them.

Did we give up stealing horses? Is there a moral to this story?

Yes: For the sore-kneed and sore at heart, it is more blessed to give love than to receive love.

"A lifelong love affair with that creature of flight we call the horse has occasionally called for deeds perhaps not in my best interest but intrinsically rewarding. I try to think of this event of more than 30 years ago not as horse rustling but as hands-on assistance to abused and neglected horses. In any case, the sorry life and gentle dying of The Old Man was a benchmark in several lives." —Bobbye S. Wicke

The $50 Bargain Horse

*For one horsewoman, an investment made at
age 12 pays off in 26 years' worth of friendship with
a special dappled gray named Cloudy.*

SHARRON MCGEE

There it was, a large chunk of Cloudy's tail protruding from the backside seam of my old yellow corduroy skirt from 1953. My granddaughter was going to participate in '50s Day at school and had asked to borrow things from "the olden days." Rummaging through the attic, I had found that skirt sprouting a tail from the rear end. The words "The End of the Tail," written above a drawing that featured the ample rump of a gray horse were fading, but still visible. I fingered the long, coarse strands and smiled, thinking, "Well, old horse, you are about to be resurrected and used again, if only briefly, by yet another generation." Those thick black hairs still hanging on the skirt had stirred memories of Cloudy, the horse of my youth, the horse of my heart.

As an only child recuperating from a succession of medical problems, I took refuge and found solace in the world and mystique of the horse. Stuffed horses in orange-crate stables, bits of vinyl and yarn crafted into tack took the place of dolls and their clothes. My wallpaper pattern was a lively hunt scene. My bookshelf was full of horse stories.

When I was well and able to participate in the normal life of a young girl in a small, rural Indiana town, the importance of the horse did not diminish. I collected horse pictures, kept scrapbooks of the great horses of the times, such as the Thoroughbred Citation, and expanded my reading to include books that dealt with breed types and training techniques, always harboring the dream of my own horse. But a dream it seemed destined to be, as my parents, a warm, supportive pair, had married young, endured the Depression and were saddled with medical bills from my illnesses. There was no money for a horse.

When I turned 12, a family friend who owned a grillroom in town asked if I'd like to wait tables for him. Eager to start saving for a horse, I went to work and, on 50 cents an hour, managed to save $50 over the next few years. I supplemented my waitress' pay by racking the empty milk-can lids on my father's milk route during the summer. A young horsewoman lived at one of Dad's stops, and we became friends. She told me about a horse that was for sale for $50. I was ecstatic! My dad went pale. He'd told me that if I found a horse for $50, I could buy him. Well, here it was, a $50 horse.

We went to look at this bargain, and I was in awe. He was an imposing animal, over 16 hands, and had a gray coat marked with dapples, accented by black points, mane and tail. How striking and grand I thought this fellow looked. Like a giant carousel horse! Never mind that his conformation showed all the signs of a draft horse ancestor somewhere. I knew he was the kind of horse that could canter with grace and power under the big top while providing a secure back for a glittering performer. I knew those heavy bones and bold, solid hooves descended from the powerful animals that so gallantly carried men in armor into lines of battle. I sensed an air about him, a presence, a dignity in his bearing.

I knew he was my horse, though he had no name. The dapples, spread generously like clouds over his expansive body, seemed to dictate the name Cloudy. He was five or six years old, his owner said, and had had very little training. Undaunted, we took Cloudy home with only a halter, a rope and how-to books for support. As I look back, I realize how lucky I was to find this particular horse. A huge, untrained animal of that age and a young girl, book smart but inexperienced— what are the odds of that combination succeeding? And yet we developed an almost magical kinship throughout the 26 years we shared.

Francesville, Indiana, is a small town, 800 people at that time, and many of the residents helped Cloudy and me in various ways. A kind farmer loaned me a saddle, and others sold me two bales of hay a week, which was all I could afford and store in the shed at the back of our yard where Cloudy lived. Other landowners sometimes stopped by to tell me that they had combined their wheat, and we were welcome to ride in their fields. The tack-shop owner kept a used saddle I liked until I could sell my bicycle and make the down payment. He also allowed me to pay off the balance in installments. The gentle lady who lived across the alley from our yard, behind Cloudy's shed, prayed for him when he developed strangles. The local vet treated him for just the cost of the medication. The kind fellow at the grain elevator struggled with the huge equipment meant to disgorge large amounts of grain until he had tamed the stream to fill my small old boiler with oats. This same nice guy would whistle as I rode by the elevator, always from a different doorway, window or catwalk in the elevator complex. I would always stop, search until I found him, and we would wave at each other. And, of course, there were my parents, who each bore a different load: Mom, who thought horses were really carnivorous, gamely trying to cope with a really big meat eater in the backyard, and Dad, struggling to keep up with the pile of manure. The gentle, sturdy gelding made many friends in Francesville over the years.

Cloudy was my friend, my playmate. We roamed the town and countryside, often playing games when we were bored. There was "the villain" game, in which I would pick an object such as a big rock, stump or ditch bank and tell my usually unflappable companion in a terror-filled voice that this object was "going to get us!" Cloudy would respond appropriately by widening his eyes, blowing, snorting and stomping at the enemy until I declared victory over the nasty wretch. (Whew! That was close, but we got him.) I rewarded his display of bravery, of course, and he, strutting with pride, accepted my praise.

"Racing vehicles" was another good game. We often rode along the wide shoulders of country roads or at the edge of fields and came in contact with vehicles halting for stop signs, accelerating away from them or pulling farm equipment at a slow pace. Cloudy loved to run and was very competitive, but tried to conceal this aspect of his nature. Deception was his game. Cloudy might appear to be minding his own business, just out for a Sunday walk, but all the while he was watching for slow-moving vehicles or those just pulling away from a stop. These Cloudy challenged. His eyes and ears would roll back to glimpse the sight and sound of the rival. If there was a slack rein and no restraint from me, he assumed the game was "on," and his pace would increase steadily, just enough to keep his nose ahead of the vehicle. I sat immobilized, no comment. But a walk became a fast walk, then a trot, an extended trot and a canter. As the vehicle accelerated, so did Cloudy, until we were flying full tilt to maintain our lead. I must admit we always won. I either pulled him in if it appeared we were going to be outrun, thereby providing him with an excuse to withdraw from competition, or the vehicle was driven by someone who knew about this game and found it fun to watch the fierce intensity of this horse as we pounded along. Cloudy grew quite smug, in fact, with his many victories and viewed powered vehicles with some disdain.

Spending so much time with me and in the company of the townspeople, Cloudy began to consider himself more than just a horse.

He learned to drink from the flow of water in the fountain in the middle of town and from the hose offered to him by someone watering a lawn. And what was so unusual when he tried to mosey up the library steps and help me return the books? Or walked into the living room when I left him standing on the porch while I took things in the house? The screen door stayed open, didn't it? Cloudy seemed a bit indignant when my mom took exception to this. His look to her as we left the room seemed to say, "No big deal, lady."

In all the years I had him, Cloudy never kicked, bit or stepped on anyone, nor refused to load or unload. Naive, I thought this was normal. Imagine my surprise when, in later years, I acquired other horses who did all of the above. Only then did I truly appreciate what a gentleman Cloudy was. He did, however, cause me trouble of another sort, particularly when he was bored. There were a few small lots around town that I used as places for him to graze and exercise. The fences were usually wrinkled and rusty. Cloudy honored them as long as I was around and walked through them when he was ready to do something else.

A ringing phone was usually the signal. Once it was the lady at the end of the block, who reported that Cloudy had pulled the clothes off her line and was now standing on her porch looking in the bedroom window! And there was the year I was attending the dance sponsored by the alumni association when a call came that Cloudy had got himself partially stuck in a full tank of water and was tangled in the fence to boot. Dressed in my formal and satin heels and in freezing weather, I rushed to the scene. Imagine this: A giant gray shadow in the moonlight, half in and half out of a water tank, forefeet tangled in wire, gazing calmly at the gathering crowd and nickering softly to me. I'd put a water tank in the corner where the fence was weakest. Cloudy knew about this weak spot, too, and, I think, was feeling neglected and bored.

He had managed to get his front feet in, through and out of the water tank and into the remaining woven wire fence. Cloudy's back legs had not been so cooperative. They had gone into the tank OK, but stubbornly would not lift out, so there he stood, patiently waiting for me to resolve his problems. No small task. Other people who had left the dance helped me get his body out of this predicament. We untangled his front feet and backed him out of the tank the way he had come in, helping him lift his back legs over the edge.

Marriage, jobs, children and college slowed our rides and private times together. We were aging. Our lives were changing. I placed him on a farm where he could run with a herd of cows. This did not work. These were beef cows, to be fattened for market, but Cloudy soon was trimming their weight as they became his harem and were herded, scattered and made to go wherever he went. Cloudy was put into a smaller pasture by himself. I think he missed life in town and began to find other things to do to amuse himself. Reaching over the fence into the pig lot, grabbing a small pig by the tail and giving him a flip was one of his favorite activities. Reaching over the fence into the garden and pulling out the onions by their tops was OK, too. Pulling all the empty fertilizer sacks out of the truck parked in his lot was fun for a while.

The last game, the one that initiated the delivery of our eviction notice, was over a dead chicken. Every day the farmer's wife crossed Cloudy's pasture to go to the henhouse. Several dead chickens had been tossed along the fence. On one fateful day, the lady swore that Cloudy reached over the fence, picked up a dead chicken by its leg and chased her, swinging the chicken wildly. The more she screamed, the more he shook the chicken. We left in disgrace. Another home had to be found for Cloudy.

An old farmer with a liking for horses agreed to board him on acres of stubble and pasture, with a small shelter up by the farmer's house. There were no chickens, pigs, cows, feed sacks or frightened wives. The old farmer was fond of Cloudy and gave me periodic reports: "I swear I've never seen a horse run like he does. I think he just runs for the hell of it." It seemed like the ideal place for a retired horse. But this home was soon in jeopardy, too. Again, while at an important social function, I got word that Cloudy was loose in Jasper County and being chased by farmers on tractors. It was just the sort of match that Cloudy would love. I could visualize the whole scenario. I raced to the farm to get information and received an apology from the old farmer, who had decided to start plowing the large field where Cloudy was running loose. The farmer had decided that he didn't need to shut the gate behind him, as Cloudy was so far away that he couldn't possibly see that it was open. Wrong! To quote the old fellow, "That old horse spied that open gate from half a mile away and came running as hard as he could for that hole. I jumped off the tractor and raced for the gate, but that rascal went flying right by me, and down the road he went." An alert had gone out and volunteers on big green tractors had taken up the pursuit. I followed the smoking trail of high-flying gravel and found tractors and Cloudy steaming in a barnyard. He was looking quite pleased with himself. It had been a fine race. And didn't he win? He was in the lot first, wasn't he?

Another farmer with a soft spot for Cloudy, though fully aware of his penchant for initiating action, offered him yet another home. This one had several old horses in residence who seemed to provide Cloudy with the company he needed. He lived there happily, I think, for several years. The magnificent dapples had disappeared, and a pure white coat stretched over his lank and rangy body. Age slowed the step, but never the spirit. His eyes still watched the gates and the moving vehicles on the road. I knew what he was thinking.

On one cool fall day, Cloudy died quietly of natural causes. He was 31 or 32. It was a very painful time. I knew that relationships like the unique one we shared are very rare.

Despite his love for freedom and a strong sense of independence, he had truly liked people. Cloudy had carried me and my two young daughters (one behind, one in front) around town and in small local parades, never once showing evidence of being the carnivore my mother feared. From this lofty perch on the big gray gelding, my oldest daughter saw the horse as I did, but my youngest tended to agree with Grandma.

This old horse was probably at least partially responsible for the fact that my oldest daughter and her family now raise and show horses. Maybe he planted the essence that is the horse into her mind and heart.

Retired now from public education and with more free time, I started going to horse shows to watch my granddaughters. The smells of leather and horse sweat, mingled with visions of horses and riders, stirred the sensuous imagery, so long dormant, of my youth and my horse. However, I thought I'd owned my last horse. But my oldest daughter, Lisa, encouraged me to take a young Arab filly from one of their Egyptian-bred mares. With only a little urging from my husband, I accepted the offer about a year ago and started all over again. It can't be the same as it was with Cloudy—that was a different time, when magic was in the air—but I think it will be good between us.

Not So Average After All

*From neglected colt to Breyer model, Dream Weaver has
filled lives with fun and hearts with love.*

SALLY MILO

I put the photo album on our dining room table and gazed out the
window at the pasture and our two Quarter Horses. Both Sonja, our
buckskin mare, and Dream Weaver, our palomino, were shaggy and
encrusted with mud. I had to chuckle to think that Dream Weaver, a
rather average gelding, was now the object of so much attention.
Donna Ewing, president of the Hooved Animal Humane Society in
Woodstock, Illinois, had just telephoned with the incredible news: Breyer Animal Creations had decided to make a plastic model of Dream
Weaver. What's more, the firm would be donating a part of the profits
of the model's sale to the Hooved Animal Humane Society. Breyer
needed pictures of Dream Weaver as soon as possible.

I opened the album, and the pages of pictures brought back a
flood of memories. The first photo was of my two young nephews
riding double on Dreamer with big smiles on their faces. The next photo
showed Dream Weaver and me. It had been taken in September 1990,
while we were on a 100-mile ride in the Shawnee National Forest in
southern Illinois. The weather was hot, but the riding had been spectacular. So had Dream Weaver's surefooted and eager performance.

There were also pictures of my son, Christopher, mounted on Dream Weaver at various horse shows, always in the ribbons and occasionally winning a first. The images recalled the time Dream Weaver represented the Hooved Animal Humane Society at the Mid-America Horse Fair in St. Charles, Illinois. The story of the gelding's life had melted the hearts of the spectators.

I then came to a photo of a starving, crippled, seven-month-old palomino colt. Taken in November 1977, it was a picture of Dream Weaver.

At that time, my husband, Tim, and I had been investigators for the Hooved Animal Humane Society for over four years. We had received a telephone call about a small herd of horses in a desperate situation. Their owner was having severe financial difficulties and needed cash. He had arranged to sell all of his horses for slaughter, and they were due to be shipped to Canada in a large stock trailer. The caller was concerned that a badly injured weanling colt he had seen could not possibly make the trip without falling down and being trampled to death. While we could not stop the sale of the horses, we did convince the owner to donate the little palomino colt to the Humane Society. We felt that euthanasia was kinder than letting him suffer an uncertain fate.

When I first saw the colt, my heart sank. He had radial nerve paralysis in his right shoulder, caused by a fall in the pasture six weeks earlier. The muscle in his right shoulder had atrophied. There was a hollow spot where muscle should have been, and the shoulder was totally paralyzed. In addition, his left leg was bent backward at the knee to such a degree that he was almost walking on his pastern. The joints in his left leg were swollen to more than twice their normal size. He was also suffering from the bone abnormality known as rickets. A veterinarian had looked at this colt a few weeks before and felt that nothing could be done to help him.

Hoping that we could give the youngster a chance, we decided to bring him home and have our own veterinarian examine him. The weanling had been kept in a filthy stall with his mother and was encrusted with manure. Because the mare was eating what little food they were given, the colt was also suffering from malnutrition. Arrangements were made for Tim to return the next day and to pick up the colt. The rest of the horses went to slaughter; the sad little weanling would never see his mother again.

The telephone was ringing when I got home from work the next day. It was my mother-in-law, Vivian, calling to tell me about a vivid dream she had had the night before. In her dream, she saw a herd of horses running across a field. Tim was with them, and suddenly a gold-colored horse, his white mane and tail flowing, broke from the herd and ran to Tim because he needed Tim's help.

I was stunned. Vivian had no way of knowing about the crippled colt that Tim would soon bring home. When I explained to Vivian the neglected colt's situation and that he would probably have to be humanely destroyed, she sharply objected. Vivian felt that her dream was a message that the colt would be all right. Before I hung up the phone, she made me promise to ask our veterinarian to give the little palomino a fighting chance.

At first, I felt that keeping my promise to Vivian was foolish. Logic told me that it would take a miracle for Dream Weaver, as I had named the colt, ever to be sound enough for light riding. Later that day, our veterinarian, whom we affectionately call "Doc," agreed with the opinion of the practitioner who had first examined the colt. Doc felt that if the youngster's paralyzed shoulder had not shown any sign of healing since the accident seven weeks before, it was unlikely that it would ever heal. He recommended euthanasia.

I knew in my heart that Doc was right, but I could not betray

Vivian's trust by breaking my promise. How could this colt heal when he was suffering from starvation? I asked Doc. He finally relented and gave the colt a two-week reprieve, making me promise that if Dream Weaver could not use both of his front legs at the end of the two weeks, he would be put down. Doc also added what I already knew: "It will take a miracle."

As the days passed, I began to feel that I had made a mistake. As much as I tried to stay detached from Dreamer, I found it was impossible. Even as badly injured as he seemed to be, he still had a good appetite, and I was amazed that he could lie down and get up on his own. The little guy had spunk and a friendly personality. As each day slipped closer to the end of his reprieve, I grew more depressed; there was no sign of improvement. The last day of the reprieve landed four days before Christmas, so Tim arranged to have the veterinarian return on Monday after the holiday to euthanatize Dream Weaver.

When we fed our horses that evening, I had to fight back tears. It seemed so unfair that this colt had never had a chance at a good life. The odds were stacked against him from the start, and now that someone wanted to help him, there was nothing more we could do. Before we went back to the house, I petted Dreamer's neck and gave him a hug. I could feel the tears slip down my cheek.

At about nine that evening, my friend Linda stopped to see Dream Weaver one last time. As we walked to the barn together, I couldn't help but notice what a beautiful night it was. A light dusting of snow swirled around our feet, and the sky was so clear you could see a billion stars. As I silently pondered the intense beauty of the night, I wondered if the events of the first Christmas had unfolded on such an evening.

When I turned on the barn lights, I couldn't believe the sight that greeted us. There was Dream Weaver standing on both front legs as if he hadn't a care in the world. There was no sign of the paralysis in his right shoulder. I have no explanation as to how that shoulder healed in just five hours, but I suddenly believed Vivian's dream was a message and that Dream Weaver would be OK.

When Doc returned on Monday, he was stunned with disbelief. He admitted that he had never seen a horse who had been so badly injured recover, let alone heal so fast. Doc felt that if the right shoulder had made such progress, the left leg would eventually straighten out and that Dreamer had a good chance of someday being sound.

The gelding frolicked in the snow the rest of that winter, and by spring he was well enough to go up for adoption. But when none of the families that came to look at him was willing to take the risk on how useful he would be, Tim and I decided to pay the adoption fee and keep Dreamer ourselves.

As the next few weeks passed, we were surprised to find that under that pale yellow hair was a glistening coat of deep gold. Dream Weaver also had a cute face, with expressive eyes and tiny ears. By the time he became a yearling, all traces of his shaky past had disappeared. The biggest surprise came slowly over time. As Dreamer matured he became totally sound, and the more we used him, the more he thrived. He was like the little engine that could. Whatever we would ask him to do, he would try his best to please us.

Dream Weaver was 14 this past April, and he has never been lame. He may never win a class at a national horse show, but he has won enough trophies and ribbons to fill my son's shelf. Dream Weaver has given my nieces and nephews enough hours of fun to fill my photo album with smiles, but most of all, he has given me enough good times to fill my life with fun, and in doing this, he has filled our hearts with love.

Yes, in most ways Dream Weaver is just an average horse, but

I feel that it's appropriate he was chosen to be a Breyer model. He represents all the "average" horses out there who individually are so special to those of us who own and care for them.

A Barnyard Brouhaha

*Nature takes its course against all odds,
including a feathered interloper.*

Betty Wahler

My friend Dorothy has a sign on her front gate that says, "Danger: Attack dog on premises." After the following incident, which I still have nightmares about, I suggested that she replace that sign with another: "Attack turkey: Trespassers, run for your life." Dorothy does have a dog—a sweet ox of a dog, who knows he could indeed be wiped out by the real terror and lord of the barnyard, Turkey Lurkey.

Turkey Lurkey hates every creature who enters his courtyard. Only Dorothy has his arrogant respect. I learned this by making the mistake of stopping to visit Dorothy when she wasn't home. Turkey Lurkey came after me with his head snaked low, like a vicious stallion. I didn't feel the need to further check out his body language. I just ran back to my car as fast as my legs could go. Faster, even.

A few months later, I made arrangements with Dorothy to breed my filly to her young stallion. It would be a new experience for both horses, neither of whom had had any previous romantic exposure. Before signing the breeding contract, I made Dorothy promise that Turkey Lurkey would be safely locked in the barn.

The day for the mating came. Dorothy is an experienced stallion manager, but she is now in her 70s and a little wobbly on her pins. I am not far behind her chronologically. If you are picturing two white-haired ladies of—let's face it—waning physical dexterity, an overwilling filly and a rambunctious young stallion, you've got it.

My little mare was giving off all the signs of being ripe to be bred, but we were a little concerned that there might be a connection problem. The stallion was quite a bit taller than the filly. We figured to counteract this by putting the stallion in a little natural pit in the breeding pen, thus positioning him lower than the mare. Dorothy assured me the turkey was safely locked in the somewhat rickety barn.

I led the filly to the breeding pen, where the stallion, Shenanigan, was waiting. Dorothy waited until his bodily instincts took over enough so that she could wash him, then led him over to the pit. "Bring the filly closer," she called. "We'll let them get acquainted first."

The filly liked that idea just fine. So did the young stallion. But the closer we got to him, the more it became apparent that Dorothy did not have as good control over Shenanigan as she was used to having with her old, experienced stallion. He was pretty much going to go where he pleased, snorting around, considering this angle and that, with Dorothy busy trying to untangle herself from the lead rope. At the same time, the filly was following her own instincts. Somehow she maneuvered so that *she* was down in the pit. She then planted herself, legs apart, tail up, waiting for the stallion to get things figured out and paid no attention to my attempts to get her out of the pit.

By this time Shenanigan, on the higher ground, was really confused. The next thing we knew, he had mounted from the side. His front legs hung uselessly over the filly's back on one side, his hind legs on the other; he was crosswise, off the ground and unable to maneuver. The filly was stoically bearing his weight. He lost his concentration.

Somehow we got them separated. Then Shenanigan tried the

head end. No go. No matter what we did, the filly always ended up in the pit, with Shenanigan up above her at an impossible angle. After four or five tries, the stallion finally figured things out. He just went down into the pit with the filly and found the right end all by himself, as Dorothy followed him, trying not to get tangled in the rope. Mother Nature was trying hard to take over, and we were about to breathe a sigh of relief when suddenly we were interrupted again. A loud ruckus arose from the barn. A turkey kind of ruckus. My heart did a double flip. I looked over to see the barn door open and Turkey Lurkey make a beeline for me, gobbling frantically.

I yelled, "Dorothy, get the turkey! He's after me!" I let go of the filly's lead rope and ran. Dorothy—bless her heart—valued my life more than her doomed stud fee, though she may have hesitated for just a second. She let go of all and ran for the turkey.

Shenanigan gave up. From my position on the other side of the fence, I could see Dorothy shooing the turkey into the barn and locking the door. The stallion and the filly, their virginal innocence still intact (or so we thought), had found some grass and were peacefully nibbling side by side. The excitement was gone, so what to do but eat?

Funny thing: Exactly 342 days later, the filly surprised us in the field with a filly of her own. On the foal's forehead is an irregular star, shaped like a turkey, with its head jutted forward and its tail feathers sticking up. Dorothy says that proves it must have happened when we were attending to Turkey Lurkey. So now she wants her stud fee. Should I pay it?

Horses entered Betty Wahler's life when she was seven and have remained for the intervening 65 years. A resident of Edgewood, Washington, Wahler has worked with a number of different breeds but, in recent years, has found Paso Finos most to her liking.

The Horse Gang
Of My Glory Days

*A reunion sparks memories of the special equine exploits
these friends experienced nearly 20 years ago.*

JAN SPRAGUE

Gangs have gotten a lot of media attention lately, but I was in a gang during high school and it probably saved me from myself. We were known simply as "the horse gang" or "Mackey's gang," after the boarding stable where the majority of us kept our horses. Mostly girls, with an occasional boy joining us, our horse gang was both a means of survival and fun.

I've been reflecting back on those days of being in a horse gang, because recently a group of us got together for the first time in 17 years. It just so happens that many of the members of our gang, now age 30-something, still live near the old stable, so we picked a weekend, made some phone calls and those of us from out of town piled into our cars to trek back to the dusty riding ring, the funky paddocks and still-used trails of our past.

Once we all got over the shock of seeing each other again and comparing notes on who had how many kids and who had been married the most or the longest, we got down to the business of horses. "Remember Pepper? Remember Caroline's crazy horse, Race Call? Remember Rusty, Lady, Lassie?" The names of those old equine friends came to us quickly, and it wasn't long before we were reconstructing those days, laughing and wondering how we had survived them.

We girls were a wild bunch on horseback. Not necessarily a part of the "in" crowd on the school grounds or popular with boys, we were just a little too rebellious to be honor-roll students. But in the saddle we shone like stars.

This was the early 1970s, a time of turmoil. For high-school-aged girls like us, the times seemed especially perplexing. Drugs, drinking and tie-dyes were rampant. Sports were out. Hippies were in. I think most of us came from homes where our parents were very busy working. There was little guidance, but even if there had been, we thought of ourselves as very nearly adults and wanted nothing more than to be treated as such.

Thank goodness for our horses. Big in heart and spirit, if lacking in papers and pedigrees, our motley crew of four-legged companions carried us and our dreams, day after day. If school was bad, boys dumb and parents ignorant, our horses were there, and they always understood.

Usually we hung out at a field or in the ring at a local stable, each of us slinging one leg over our horse's withers, talking like cowboys on a break from riding herd. The conversation was seldom about horses. It focused, of course, on the latest gossip. But sooner or later, someone would begin practicing pole bending or running barrels, and then we would all join in, taking turns, trying to outdo each other. The cares and worries that often seem to overburden a young person blew away with the dust churned up by our horse's flying hooves.

I'll never forget the many rides we took across town to the horse shows. In our town, there was one formally organized horse group and one official showring. It was located next to a sewage-treatment plant, on the other side of the freeway from where we lived. Because we were mostly kids from working-class parents, we didn't have the saddles, horse trailers and other fancy gear, but that didn't stop us from entering gymkhana competitions.

To get to these shows meant rising at dawn to feed our horses, groom them meticulously, throw on the hackamores we always used (as well as a bareback pad to keep our legs from getting plastered with horsehair), and setting off on a ride that took us from our county outskirts past trim little suburban homes with their sidewalks and curbs, across busy boulevards and the freeway, over school grounds and then into the country again. Our steady mounts would calmly tackle the roadways, but as we drew nearer to the show grounds, the sights and smells would cause them to toss their heads, open their eyes wide and flare their nostrils. They'd prance with excitement, and we would enter the place looking like the Dalton Brothers or Jesse James and his gang—wild, dusty and rarin' to go.

Often, even after carrying us the considerable distance to the show, our horses would win. I still remember the first time my friend Lorie showed her very green Appaloosa mare, Dusty, in a single pole race. It was the only class where we had figured out what we were supposed to do. Dusty raced as if she had been competing all of her life. With a stout kick from Lorie, the mare took off like a jet. She cornered the pole perfectly and came flying home for a big finish, Lorie's braids flying straight out behind her. No other rider that day could touch their time, but Dusty and Lorie were later disqualified because Lorie had not ridden with a saddle.

My forte became the trotting race. Lacking in riding skills and having a gimpy-legged, 18-year-old Thoroughbred named Dixie at the time, I knew that this was one competition we had a chance of winning. Dixie loved to trot, and I had taught myself to post to keep up with her long strides. We'd trot everywhere we went, proving that if you stick to one thing, you will eventually do it well. When show day came and it was time for the trotting race, people knew Dixie by sight. "That's the trotting horse—look at them go!" Those words made me smile inside and out.

If only we had tackled our school studies with the same enthusiasm we invested in our riding. After hanging over the rails of the showrings and carefully watching the more experienced riders, we would go home and duplicate their moves, step for step. We helped each other out with pointers, criticisms and ideas, and even shared tack when one of us in the group found that her equipment was lacking. Little by little, our equestrian skills improved, and so did our horses.

Among our favorite mounts was little Pepper, a wonder of a barrel horse, who wouldn't load into a trailer unless Suanne rode her into it and then rode her out again to unload. Because of that, Suanne had to have an open trailer. My horse at the time, a tough little half-Morgan mare named Chick, would walk into a trailer calmly enough, but unloading was always exciting. First you prayed, then you untied the horse and stood back while she exited at 90 miles an hour, often flipping herself in the process.

Liz had a Quarter Horse–Thoroughbred mare named Lady, who certainly did not live up to her name when it came to getting into the showring. Usually, it took two or three of us hanging onto the bridle to keep the horse on earth, while Liz held on for dear life and we guided the mare through the gate. After one or two gymkhana classes, Liz would resort to backing Lady into the arena. They almost always won.

There was also Caroline's crazy gray horse, Race Call, who would usually take off during our frequent trail rides. A beautiful animal, he actually had a pit in his head; perhaps that accounted for his craziness. The best method Caroline had for stopping him was to head him up a steep incline. We'd all wait at the bottom, yelling out advice when it seemed appropriate and chatting away while we waited for them to rejoin us.

On the backs of these fine steeds, we covered many miles. When we went on a trail ride, it wasn't the wimpy stuff I do today. Often we'd ride a good hour or so, just picking up friends on the way. Then we'd set off on a sojourn to a place we'd always wondered about. In those days you were unlikely to run into a fence, and if you did, there was always a gate to go through. The trails were limitless.

Though we may not have realized it at the time, the hours we spent traversing the countryside were responsible for the horses' good physical condition. Their own horse sense also ensured their well-being. For instance, one summer after seeing the Walt Disney movie *Run, Appaloosa, Run!* we decided to hold our own suicide race. We designed a challenging cross-country course, complete with jumps, streams and a steep downhill gallop. One person would hold the timer, while we took turns trying to outrace each other—riding bareback, of course. The horses seemed to think the idea of this event was to outsmart their riders. They knew how to avoid the jumps, stop at the stream and refuse to go down the steep parts. They were smarter than we were then, and we were probably better off for it.

Yet whatever we asked of them, they tried to do, even when we decided to expand our horizons by taking up English riding. This "new" approach to horsemanship had us all stymied at first. But by reading books, trading in our hackamores for snaffles and passing down the knowledge one of us gleaned from her professional lessons, we all were soon practicing French braids and building rickety jumps.

How we would get those horses to jump! Even today, I think back on our crude methods and wonder how we accomplished as much as we did. For the most part, we would simply point a horse to a pole balanced on top of a pair of three-foot barrels and just expect him to jump it. Remarkably, he usually did. I guess we lived and breathed with those horses so much, they not only trusted us, but could read our minds to a certain degree. Because we all couldn't afford English saddles, we'd share the few available or just jump bareback, which felt more comfortable.

You have to understand that we were all first-generation horsepeople, and so everything was new to us. Our parents didn't ride, nor did they care too much about horses. But they loved us, and so were understanding of our consuming passion to be with our horses. I think there was some vicarious thrill, too, when we all took up horse showing. Often my mom would appear at shows with fried chicken to make sure we were well nourished, then she would join the other mothers as they hid their eyes and gasped while we rode hell-bent for leather.

Though our exploits sound extraordinary, be assured that these horses were the most loved and prized friends we had. They held us together like glue. They supplied us with a form of recreation and companionship and were the best counselors we had. When I think back today on all the time lavished on my horse, I feel a certain regret that I cannot afford to spend as many hours on my horse today.

I still ride, but it is wedged in between the multitude of chores I must accomplish each day, including the care of two children. I am a more polished rider today, with the proper riding clothes, a trainer, a horse who is showing potential for the type of competition I only dreamed of in the "old" days. I have taken up more illustrious forms of riding than in my youth. Now I practice dressage and hope to show my young Thoroughbred gelding in eventing.

But when I see the kids in our area on their grade horses, when I see them gathered together in a circle, talking, when the local gymkhana group holds its meets and the youngsters are trying their hardest to shine like stars on their ponies, I feel a sense of pride for them. "Go for it!" I want to shout to them, "Ride those horses!" My thoughts drift back to my horse gang. Back then we were misfits, struggling with identity crises, but we were special when we were on our horses. We got our first jobs so we could afford the best saddles, the best gear, liniment, fly spray and grain and the latest horse fad. Nothing was too good for our best friends. And make no mistake about it, we all knew who that was. It was the animal who shared our secrets and absorbed our tears into his coat, whose ears were always tuned to our voices. It was the beautiful, sleek creature with the long legs and big brown eyes. Our horses were our friends, and I don't think I'll ever know that kind of partnership again.

Two Changes Of Heart

When an imposing Saddlebred learned how to be a horse,
he became a treasured companion.

Judy Berkley Clark

He was the kind of horse my husband likes—big, bold and bad. Singing Hills Headmaster stood attentively in the cross ties while his sweeping tail was unbraided and finger-combed. In the half-light of the barn's aisleway, with his muscles tensed under a gleaming chestnut coat, his eyes staring intently, the 17-hand American Saddlebred seemed aglow with inner fire. A veteran of the national show circuit and near the end of his career, the gelding was still a tower of spirit and beauty. He was like a Rolls Royce seen from a distance. I couldn't actually hear the engine, but I could feel the hum.

"I really like this horse," my husband whispered to me, in what I recognized as his price-haggling voice. I was glad. It was the first interest Mike had shown in a horse since his beloved Gemini, a huge Tennessee Walker mare with a sublimely smooth ride and the personality of a rhinoceros, had injured a coffin bone and started a lengthy and uncertain convalescence.

I was glad, too, that I wouldn't be handling this monster. Though a newcomer to the world of horses, I could at least recognize an animal that was too much for me. I trusted Mike's judgment about horses, but I was uneasy about Headmaster. I sensed that behind all the gloss and glamour there was a horse that was different from any I'd encountered so far, and I resolved to stay out of his way. Besides, my sweet-tempered Quarter Horse, Kid, still had plenty to teach me. Between Headmaster and Kid, however, I was to learn a lot about first impressions.

In the months that followed Headmaster's arrival, he boorishly confirmed my initial fears about him. If I passed his stall, he would lay back his ears, snake his long neck and point his front hooves. If I haltered him to groom him, I was the dope on the rope, dragged at the end of the lead wherever he chose to go. And if I tried to ride him in the relative safety of the indoor arena, he'd feel my inexperienced hands and balk or whirl. Obviously, Headmaster didn't think much of me, and I heartily returned the sentiment!

Kid—short for Don'tcha Kid Me—was stabled next to Headmaster. A well-schooled Quarter Horse, he had been ridden and shown by experienced riders. But when I acquired Kid, he became the teacher, a role he played with gentlemanly patience. He was never soured by my mistakes, and as I learned more, he willingly gave more. Though Kid was a good, honest, workmanlike horse, he was aloof by nature. At his most affectionate, he might nuzzle my neck or hand briefly, and he was coolly indifferent to other horses.

At first, Kid seemed to survey Headmaster's bad manners with prissy disdain, but his reserve was soon replaced by active hostility. All his sterling virtues disappeared whenever he was close enough to deliver a kick or sink his teeth into the big horse. In short, my Mr. Cool became Mr. Hyde in the presence of his new stablemate.

Mike, however, was thrilled with his equine acquisition. Though he'd been riding since childhood and breaking and training since his early teens, it was Mike's first experience with a Saddlebred's versatility of movement. Each of Headmaster's gaits has a dozen variations, and Mike worked up a little routine to show off the Saddlebred's fancy footwork. After a minuet-like jog, a fiery high-stepping trot, a ground-covering pace, an elegant rack and a merry-go-round-horse canter-in-place would come the grand finale—Headmaster rearing up and executing four or five spectacular leaps with Mike on his back. After one particularly impressive display, Mike remarked admiringly, "That darn horse has more moves than a bag of snakes." And that's how Headmaster acquired a nickname that stuck—Jake the Snake.

That summer, Mike thought our horses would benefit from a change of scene and the company of other pasturemates, so Kid and the newly christened Jake were turned out in a pasture with a dozen other horses. That's when the impressions I'd formed of the pair began to alter radically. Except for his uncharacteristic hostility toward Jake, Kid seemed like a mild-mannered Goody Two Shoes, but in the pasture he promptly established himself as a vigorous herd boss. His chest and hindquarters became massive from continually cutting and dogging the other geldings and shepherding the mares, duties he performed with his usual solemn efficiency. He ran the whole show as if he'd been doing it all his life.

In contrast, Jake the Snake, who had come on as the baddest of the bad and who had terrorized me, turned out to be a wimp. Though he towered above all the other horses, he was at the bottom of the pecking order, kicked and bitten at every turn. One tiny vindictive pony loved to run under Jake's belly and, though he had to stretch to do it, give the big horse a kick in the slats.

Our attempts to relieve this abuse by keeping Jake stabled resulted in kindling wood. After his heady taste of freedom, Jake would bash through anything that kept him from his rough companions. Though I was no fan of Jake's, I hated to see the treatment he was enduring and asked Mike about it. "Jake doesn't know how to be a horse," he explained. "He's never been with his own kind, and he's got to learn the hard way." And though it was difficult, the big horse seemed intent on changing his ways.

We watched in amusement as Jake learned to roll. For weeks he stared quizzically as the other horses scratched their backs. After he finally made the attempt himself, there was just no stopping him. He was constantly squirming up a cloud of dust, waggling his legs in the air and looking awfully pleased with himself.

With equal fervor, Jake pursued friendship. Though his goony behavior was constantly met with a barrage of kicks, he refused to accept outsider status. His determination to be part of the Family of Horse, at any cost, was touching. Finally Nicky, a playful youngster, started warming up to Jake, teaching him mutual grooming, mock fighting and a game they played for hours, the lip-grabbing game. At the age of 16, Jake was acting like a playful colt. Kid, four years younger, acted like a crabby old fogey and continually rebuffed Jake's overtures of friendship.

While all this socialization and sorting out was going on, however, something was amiss, something we didn't catch until it was too late. After two months in the pasture, a change he obviously relished despite his rough initiation, Jake's weight suddenly plummeted. Like most Saddlebreds, he was lightly fleshed, but seemingly overnight he dropped 200 pounds. His beautiful long neck wasting, his ribs and hipbones protruding, Jake stood listlessly in the pasture, his eyes dull, his fire quenched. He seemed to have lost interest in the life he had so recently been discovering.

Repeated visits from the veterinarian failed to turn up an answer. Jake's teeth were checked, he was dewormed and his blood was drawn and sent to the lab, but nothing was amiss. On the third visit, still with no clues to the problem, the veterinarian was stroking Jake's glossy hide where it lay over bony ribs. "I just don't get it," the practitioner said. "This isn't the coat of a sick animal."

Abruptly, his hand halted. Thoughtfully he withdrew his palm and looked beneath it. There on the horse's hide was a round flat welt. Half a minute later, another appeared near it. "Hives!" crowed the veterinarian triumphantly. "He's got hives!"

Bewildered by the turn of events, but encouraged by the veterinarian's jubilant tone of voice, I asked, "What does that mean?" Still mulling over this new development, the practitioner replied slowly, "Something's got him stressed out—possibly feeding time. Either he's not getting enough to eat, or the presence of all these other horses is so stressful that he's not getting the benefit of the food."

The veterinarian's prescription was to take Jake out of the pasture morning and evening and feed his grain and alfalfa to him in a quiet spot away from the herd. This duty, like most doctoring chores around our place, fell to me. And during that convalescence, when he was at low ebb, I came to know the real Jake, a horse so unlike any other that I had misunderstood him from the start.

My change of heart began when I realized that Jake had his horse signals hopelessly crossed. When he flattened his ears and pounded his hooves, he wasn't showing aggression, but giving me an enthusiastic Jake-style welcome. When he snaked out his long neck, it wasn't for hostility but for hugs, as he pulled me into a close embrace, or his favorite trick—grabbing my shoulder in his teeth to suck on my shirt and gaze soulfully at my face. (Mike and I always have shirts with saliva epaulettes!)

As Jake's weight and energy returned, I also learned about his endless curiosity. Everything within reach—rakes, riding crops, boots, hoof picks, everything—had to be picked up in his mouth and examined for its entertainment potential. The light switch outside the tack-room door, when his long upper lip could reach it, had to be clicked on and off repeatedly while he stares at the flickering light bulb like an equine Edison.

Mike himself was the object of Jake's curiosity. More than once, hurrying past the big horse without giving Jake a proper greeting, Mike was lifted by the shirt collar and dangled in the air until a more acceptable salutation was forthcoming.

The turnabout that was occurring between Jake and me was of interest to Kid. When Jake was given his private feedings, Kid would come to the fence, with his favorite mares tagging along, to survey the special treatment. I feared that jealousy, the one emotion Kid had previously shown himself capable of, would be a particular problem, but, paradoxically, he began to respond to Jake's attempts at friendship.

Mike liked to dismiss their growing intimacy by saying that "Kid just wants to be there when the carrots are passed out," but in the year that followed, we watched the special privileges that Kid allowed only to Jake and the inexplicable bond that formed between them. They were never far from one another; they shared food and their personalities have merged and mingled. Kid taught Jake how to be a horse—Jake now acted like a self-important second-in-command. And Jake taught Kid the ways of friendship—Kid became affectionate and playful in a way he never was in the pre-Jake days. Clearly Kid, like me, had a change of heart about Jake, and finally even Mike had to admit, "Those two are like peanut butter and jelly."

Then came the day when the veterinarian pronounced Mike's beloved Tennessee Walker sound again, and we were a family with an extra horse, faced with the question, "What do we do with Jake?" I thought of how he rubbed his back legs together like a giant cricket, how he flapped his lips—*whop, whop*—like two oven mitts clapping, thought of how many days we'd used the phrase, "Guess what Jake did today?" I thought of how different it was to ride Jake when I understood all his bluff and baloney—and I thought it would be miserable for Kid and me to part with him. That day, I became the owner of a second horse.

I had feared and disliked Jake at first, but I came to treasure him, and I wonder, at times, if my own emotional journey with that big, complicated horse didn't somehow contribute to Kid's initial hostility and subsequent acceptance and love of Jake. If so, it epitomizes one of the great mysteries about horses—why do they choose to empathize with human feeling? It's one thing that they put their strength and beauty at our service, but to feel that a communion of heart and mind has occurred is an awesome privilege.

Jake and Kid have enlightened and enriched my life, but they're also friends of mine who are just plain fun. Looking out the window to the lower pasture where the sun is gleaming gold on their coats, I can see that Jake has cajoled Kid into playing the lip-grabbing game.

Won't Daddy Be Surprised!

*When one family unexpectedly adopted
a wild burro, no one imagined the trials they would face or
the rewards they would receive.*

Pam Eberhardt-Kuhlman

I have always been positive that if a creature from the next galaxy needed something to eat and a place to sleep, it would find its way to our house. Little furry creatures (and some large ones, too) have come great distances just to share our hospitality.

Besides adopting the usual stray cats and an abandoned dog, I actually purchased an abused and paranoid horse in order to give her the peace of a loving home. Here was a 1,000-pound creature who was afraid of her own shadow, not to speak of bicycles, kids and cars. With time and patience, and a home in our backyard, the mare we now call Odyssey had quieted down and almost grown accustomed to the sound of the neighbor's lawn mower.

My husband, Chris, whose only prior horse experience was a pony ride as a child, was just about used to the family's collection of animals, which also includes chickens, ducks and geese, when he brought home a newspaper clipping for me to read. The article told of the Bureau of Land Management's intent to bring wild mustangs and burros to the Lake County (Illinois) Fairgrounds so they could be adopted. The article listed an address in Milwaukee to write to for an application. Though Chris gave his nod of approval when I sent for the form, in the back of his mind, he was thinking there was no way we would ever be able to adopt a wild burro.

A few days after I had mailed the completed application to the BLM, I received a call from Alexandria, Virginia, the home office of the adoption program. The purpose of the call was to make sure that my husband and I had proper facilities to care for a burro. The caller also said that the BLM was bringing only 50 burros into Illinois, and that it had already received more adoption applications than that. When I told my husband, he smiled and said, "See, I told you so." Nonetheless, I kept our daughter, Elizabeth, home from school that Friday in late April so she could go with me to see the wild mustangs and burros. What an experience it would be for her—and for me, too.

We arrived at the Lake County Fairgrounds early to watch people select their animals. Those whose applications had been submitted before mine were given lottery numbers and the opportunity to choose a horse or burro. Elizabeth and I, along with several others wishing to adopt, sat and waited, on the chance that not everyone whose application had been accepted had actually shown up.

The freezing-cold morning inched its way to afternoon and an announcement came over the loudspeakers that not all of the adopters had come to the fairgrounds and a new lottery was going to be formed from the list of late applicants. When the hat with the numbers was offered, my daughter squeezed through the crowd and selected the second number for a burro. We could hardly believe we were going to get a chance to adopt one of these cute animals. The selection process wasn't easy, but we finally chose a two-year-old jack. "Won't Daddy be surprised?" Elizabeth asked.

Only one predicament remained: how to get him home. It took several calls before I finally found someone with a horse trailer who was willing to load and haul a wild animal. Though the ride home was uneventful, the horse trailer carrying our new acquisition could not be backed through the gate across our driveway. It was up to Chris and me to get our little captive out of the trailer and down the 400-foot driveway to the back pasture.

We put another lead rope on the halter so as to have one person on each side to control the frightened burro. After he dragged the two of us around the front yard for a while, Chris figured out that if we stayed at the burro's hindquarters, we could drive him forward while using the lead ropes to steer him. It worked. He was home at last.

Through all the flurry of getting our burro into the back corral, Odyssey watched from her stall window in the barn. She was having a fit, thinking that her quiet domain was being invaded. To her, the burro represented competition for love and food.

Exhausted, Chris and I sat outside the fence and watched as our burro tried to hide behind some trees. We had a long way to go in gaining his confidence. We knew that by the time fall and bad weather came, we wanted to have him "domesticated" enough to walk on a lead at command and stay in a stall, neither of which he had experienced before. From the relatively short time we had just spent with him, we realized how much work it was going to take. My husband named the burro Moses, saying that this was a biblical experience.

Every day I went out into Moses' corral and sat on the ground under a tree. I took a loaf of bread with me each time and tossed pieces of it in his direction. He became confident enough to walk over to the pieces and sniff them. After some time, Moses tasted the bread and decided that this stuff was pretty good. I knew I had him then. Now I could use this "treat" to get him to accept me.

In the meantime, I took some well-meant but bad advice from a neighbor who also has horses in his backyard. He said we should put

Odyssey and Moses together in the same corral. After a bit of kicking and nipping, he said, they would become great friends.

It was a near disaster. As soon as Moses and Odyssey were in the corral that formerly had been hers and hers alone, the mare took off after the burro with teeth bared and hooves flying. Moses dashed through the welded wire and electric fences. Nothing was going to stop him from getting away from this crazy horse. Yet much to our surprise, once he was away from danger, he stopped and began munching on our front lawn. It took both Chris and me a bit of doing to get Odyssey settled down and back into the barn and to return Moses to the corral. With that accomplished, we knew that we were going to have to spend our next paycheck and weekend on fencing in another pasture just for Odyssey.

Once Moses had his own space, I spent even more hours sitting on the ground, offering him bread. Quite unexpectedly one day, he came up to me and began sniffing my shoes, my hair and my face. I was excited and a bit afraid. After all, Moses may be cute, but he is wild and weighs 500 pounds. And there I was sitting on the ground at his feet. The burro never tried to hurt me, however. Apparently my plan to win his trust through patience—and bread—had worked.

While seated on the ground, I also accustomed the burro to being touched. I fed him bread with one hand while my other held a bit of hay toward his front shoulder. Slowly and gently, I touched his shoulder with the hay. Eventually, Moses allowed me to stroke his neck and forehead with the hay. The first time he let me touch him without the hay in my hand felt like a real accomplishment. From there out, he began trusting us more and more.

The spring days were turning more into summer, and it was time to call the veterinarian to give Moses his booster shots—he had received his initial immunizations after he was captured for adoption—

and a deworming paste. Living in an arid part of the country and free to move from place to place, burros do not become infected with parasites. However, once they live in a more humid environment and are kept with other animals in a relatively small area, a deworming program becomes an essential part of their management.

I tried desperately to gain enough control over Moses so I would be able to restrain him for the veterinarian, but time was not on my side. Somehow, Moses had gotten his lead rope off his halter. Part of his training included leaving the lead on him so that when he stepped on it and consequently put pressure on the noseband of his halter, he would learn to stop. This would have also made it easier (in theory) to grab him and hold him for the veterinarian.

The day our practitioner arrived, he decided to first take care of Odyssey in the barn before tackling Moses. Up to this point, I thought I had been successful in getting the burro to trust me, but I think a fear of veterinarians is born into all four-legged creatures. Moses was hiding behind a tree and would not come out.

Undaunted, the veterinarian got a lariat out of his truck and ran around the corral after Moses, holding the rope high above his head. On his second try, he got the lariat over Moses' head but accidentally dropped the end of the rope. The two of us ran around the corral and finally managed to pick up the end of the rope and wrap it once around a tree. With each turn, I took up the slack in the rope until Moses' nose was just about into the bark. The veterinarian carefully came up to Moses' hindquarters and got the two shots into him. He then put the deworming paste into the burro's mouth. However, instead of releasing Moses when his ministrations were complete, he put the lead back on him and tied him to the tree. He told me to leave the burro tied to the tree for a few hours to teach him that his captors were the ones in control.

Well, as much as I depend on my veterinarian's expert opinions, in this case, I felt his training method was not the one I wanted to use. I felt that I could accomplish the same ends by using a kinder and more trust-evoking means, even though my methods would probably take a lot longer time and require twice the amount of patience.

Step by step and day by day, Moses came closer and closer. He learned that he could be touched by us and not be hurt or frightened. He learned not to drink from puddles on the ground but out of buckets and troughs. He learned quickly that we fed him, and he soon began to call us at breakfast and dinnertime. The first time we heard him "hee haw," we all broke up laughing. It was an unusual sound for suburbia.

Soon we began teaching Moses to walk on the lead. Standing before him with a treat in hand, we rewarded him when he took steps forward. In time, he took more and more steps, until we were able to walk him out of the corral and into the backyard. We walked him up to the barn and tried to get him used to the sounds and smells there.

Chris was the first to get Moses into a stall. At first, the burro kicked the stall boards and snorted. But each time we put him into the stall, we rewarded him with fresh hay and a little sweetfeed. We left him in the barn only a few minutes each time, lengthening the stay until finally one cold, rainy fall day, we put him in the barn and left him there. He realized that for the first time in his life, it was raining and he wasn't getting wet.

During this time, Odyssey had been adjusting to having Moses in the barn with her. They sniffed at each other through the partition that divided their stalls. During the day, when they were turned out in separate pastures, they kept an eye on each other through the fence. We did, however, have to treat them like siblings who easily become jealous of one another. Whenever one was given a carrot or an apple, the other had to receive the same treat so as not to feel left out.

Chris and I procrastinated putting Moses and Odyssey into the same corral until the property next to ours was sold and construction began. We realized that when a bulldozer began working on the fence line just a few feet from Moses' corral, we would have to move him in with Odyssey, just to get him away from the terrible noise.

When the fateful day could no longer be postponed, Chris put Moses in Odyssey's corral, and then I led the mare into the enclosure. Odyssey did her normal routine, first rolling, then getting up, kicking, bucking and running around with her tail held high in the air. Moses just stood to the one side, watching her, the whites of his eyes showing. Odyssey did not go after Moses, however. She had her fun but never tried to hurt him.

Slowly, Moses began walking toward her and she toward him. Suddenly, they touched noses. Moses jerked back in fear and snorted. Then he realized that she hadn't hurt him. They sniffed at each other again and touched noses once more. Chris and I, standing at the gate, breathed a sigh of relief.

Daily turnouts have become a joy to watch. Moses and Odyssey sometimes roll at the exact same time, get up and shake like wet dogs, and then buck and kick as they run around the corral in opposite directions. They play with each other, pretending to bite, but purposely missing contact with flesh by several feet. Every evening, when Chris and I walk out to the corral to lead the two of them into the barn, we smile. Moses and Odyssey are there waiting for us at the gate, standing side by side.

After a particularly hard winter, spring burst upon us. April was here once more, bringing with it the Canada geese and red-winged blackbirds and the need for Moses to see the farrier for hoof trimming and the veterinarian for castration. From the beginning of the burro's lessons on being touched, I had tried to get him used to having his legs and feet handled. We had even gotten to the point where he would allow me to pick up each hoof and tap gently on the sole. When the farrier arrived for that fateful first trim, I learned that my lessons were well worth it. According to the farrier, he had less of a problem trimming Moses than he'd had in the past trimming foals for the first time.

Moses was equally well-behaved for the veterinarian when he came to geld him. The practitioner arrived first thing in the morning, remembering the time he had had with Moses the year before. I think he must have felt that he wanted to get the hardest part of his day over first. He was pleasantly surprised, however. Moses was in his stall, calmly munching his breakfast, and he paid little attention to the veterinarian's ministrations. In just a short while, the surgery was completed, and our veterinarian complimented us on how tame Moses had become in just one year. He also certified for the BLM that the burro was healthy and well cared for. Now Moses' title would be granted to us as his adopters.

Chris and I are now training Moses to accept a bit and bridle. He is progressing well. Next will be sandbags on his back for weight and finally a saddle. We haven't decided yet which one of us will be the first to sit on his back. Chris did say, however, much to my surprise, that he'd be willing to do this again someday when we get a bigger place. I couldn't believe my ears.

Adopting a wild burro isn't for everyone. I know that we could not have handled a wild mustang. But if you have a lot of time on your hands and are willing to tame an animal with trust and love, then adopting a wild burro can be one of the most satisfying and rewarding times you'll ever enjoy. And, by the way, our certificate of title arrived just the other day. We framed it and have it hanging very proudly on the living room wall.

A True Endurance Test

A helicopter airlifts an Arabian horse to safety when he stumbles from a rocky, mountain trail.

By Matthew Mackay-Smith, DVM, with Jennifer Johnson

For quite some time, Denise Shepard's endurance-rider friends had been trying to convince her that her Arabian stallion, Mintyfa (otherwise known as "Goat") was a natural for long-distance competition. So when the Fort Valley 50, held on Virginia's Massanutten Mountain, rolled around in November, Denise decided that she and Goat would finally give endurance competition a try. As she trailered her horse from northeastern Pennsylvania, Denise was optimistic about finishing the ride, even though she was well aware that the Fort Valley 50 is considered one of the most rugged rides on the East Coast.

From the moment they left the starting point that Sunday, Denise and Goat made steady progress along the trail and stayed in the top third of competitors. At about 40 miles, they came to an area of rock fall, where myriad boulders and smaller pieces of the mountainside had tumbled down the steep incline. For safety's sake, Denise and her riding companions decided to dismount and walk alongside their horses until they reached less precarious footing on the trail. Eventually, Denise's two friends remounted, but the novice competitor wasn't comfortable with the uneven terrain so she continued to walk with her horse. As her friends trotted out of sight, another competitor unexpectedly came up behind Denise and Goat. Startled, the Arabian stallion jumped sideways and landed about two feet below the trail. A step or two would have put him safely back on course, but Goat pulled away from Denise as she tried to coax him back onto the trail. In the process, he scrambled his way from bad footing to impossible terrain.

Denise's concern for her horse temporarily conquered her acrophobic nature, and she went to his rescue. But when she attempted to urge him back up toward the trail, he hurled himself onto the rock fall and began skittering and flipping down the mountain. Finally, after traveling about 1,000 feet—and 600 vertical feet down—from the trail, he came to a crunching halt.

In a state of shock, Denise began calling for help. Allan Geoffrion, another competitor, heard her cries and stopped his horse. He went down to see if he could help, but after assessing the situation, he realized that it was going to take a team effort to get the stallion out of his predicament. Geoffrion tied his bandanna to a twig to mark the spot where Goat was marooned and headed off to Heishman's Meadow, the next checkpoint on the ride. Upon arriving, he described the emergency, and all available hands began to mobilize.

Marc Read, MD, an area physician who was helping with the Fort Valley 50, joined Denise's son, Shawn Eller, ride manager Tom Sites and volunteer radioman "Sandy" Sanderson to head to the mountain to evaluate the situation. They found an emotional Denise watching over her stallion, who, miracle of miracles, appeared to be in relatively good condition. After somersaulting and flip-flopping down the rocky mountainside, Goat had only a minimal amount of visible damage and use of all four limbs. But with each attempt his rescuers made to lead him to more solid footing, the Arabian would struggle and slip farther away from the trail. Eventually, he ended up straddling a teetering boulder. With some rope they had brought, the four men stabilized Goat and the rock as best they could.

After finishing my duties as the ride's head veterinarian, I assembled emergency medication and bandage materials and headed off to see what else we could do for the indestructible equine. I just happened to have my brand-new chain saw and a jug of water I'd grabbed for the workers. Then a half dozen of us, many of whom had just finished the challenging ride, four-wheeled our way into the mountain to within a half mile of the trail. Shouldering our gear, we quickly headed toward the horse.

Not wanting to frighten Goat, we carefully worked our way down what I believe was the most hazardous rock fall I have ever been on. When we finally reached him, I realized that he was going into shock. His pulse was at 90 beats per minute, very weak, and his blood pressure was very low. Additionally, scant gut sounds, cold ears and a clammy body all pointed to the fact that Goat was experiencing cardio-vascular collapse. To combat the progressive ravages of shock and injury, I gave him dexamethasone phosphate to protect his adrenal glands and stabilize his electrolyte balance. To thwart the destructive effects of prostaglandins produced in response to wounds and contusions, I injected flunixin meglumine (Banamine). The combination would also combat pain and depression. Initially, I gave him no more than an even chance of surviving.

After as thorough an examination as I could manage under the adverse conditions, I determined that Goat's multiple wounds were superficial. He had not broken any leg bones. The blood that periodically passed through his nostrils appeared to be from a broken nose, which was painful but not serious. We bandaged the horse's lower legs to stop the bleeding, and then, using rocks, dirt and leaves, we built a platform in front of him. As he was beginning to show signs of giving up, we carefully maneuvered him, leg by leg, onto this small island of solid ground.

Satisfied that we had made his position less precarious, we radioed for more veterinary assistance and materials, and I began looking for a way to walk the horse out. No matter how I searched the mountainside, however, I could not find a suitable path.

Presently, our requested backup arrived in the form of veterinarians Suzanne Michel, from the Delaware Equine Center in Cochranville, Pennsylvania, and Raymond Hyde, of Lincoln, Virginia. They had brought us fresh supplies, including five gallons of water, hay, electrolytes and additional medicine.

At the sight of the water, Goat brightened a little and drank a few sips. We were relieved at this sight because he had become very lethargic and was acting very uncomfortable, wringing his head, stamping his feet and lifting his tail. We had been concerned that a full bladder was the source of his discomfort (during endurance rides, stallions are often reluctant to urinate). Additionally, we knew that his guts had shut down, increasing his pain.

At about 7:30 p.m., I left the stabilized horse in the capable hands of the veterinarians who would be monitoring him throughout the night and went back to give Denise a firsthand report. She was relieved to learn that the stallion was still alive but alarmed that I had been unable to find a way to lead him safely back up the mountainside. "The only way to bring him out now is with a helicopter," I said. "It has been done before, so the techniques are known. But we have to find a helicopter and somebody willing to fly it."

Then I went on to the ride awards dinner to report to the others. There was a flurry of activity at this news, as virtually all those assembled began to organize the details of this extraordinary rescue effort. Kim Shelton, from the Richmond area, spent the night coordinating the details and started home with her horses after daybreak on Monday. She had had a hunch that finding a helicopter was going to be difficult, so she called the viewer crisis-assistance service at Channel 12 News in Richmond, Virginia, to see if anyone there might be able to advise us. This set into motion a chain of inquiry and persuasion that eventually led Virginia Gov. Gerald Baliles to declare the situation a limited state of emergency, allowing the Virginia National Guard to send up a tactical helicopter and crew.

Meanwhile, an appropriate sling and additional medication, provided by the Marion duPont Scott Equine Medical Center in Leesburg, Virginia, were on their way to the mountain with Steve Hummer, the hospital's manager, who had also served in the First Air Cavalry in Vietnam as an emergency rescue-team manager.

By 2 p.m. Monday, we were ready to carry out our mission. Though the prospect of airlifting a horse seems rather daunting, we discovered that the procedures involved are actually straightforward. You tranquilize the horse enough to put a sling on him; then two to three minutes before the helicopter arrives, you anesthetize the animal so that he goes down in a heap. The greatest problem is usually finding a cable long enough to reach from the helicopter to the horse. If the line is too short, the rescue team must work in a tremendous prop wash, and the margin for error gets tighter and tighter. Knowing that we wouldn't have much room to spare on the mountainside, the rescuers there began to cut trees to give us every available inch of space.

When the helicopter crew arrived, we found that the lift strap they had was only 60 feet long. They were unwilling to add cable or chain they had not tested, so we debated what to do. Meanwhile, the veterinarians who were with Goat were proceeding to put the sling on him. We radioed up to tell them that the National Guard officer in charge of the rescue was coming up in a truck to assess the situation before he gave the go-ahead for the helicopter to go in. There was a long, disturbing pause, and then the radio crackled with the response, "The horse is anesthetized, and you'll either have to come and get him now or drop off more anesthetic. We have only enough to keep him out for a half hour."

With no more medication on hand, I looked at Charlie Davis, the helicopter pilot, and said, "I guess we have to go now."

With that, Charlie started the helicopter's engines and we headed for the ravine. As I hung out the window, trying to catch sight of the crew below, I realized that the area was far more forbidding than it looked from the ground. Nevertheless, we located our friends and Goat, and Charlie began inching his way in, clearing the tops of the surrounding trees by scant inches.

Down below, everyone seemed to be organized despite the terrible wind we created and the flying debris. Still, even with repeated maneuverings, the end of the strap would come no closer than six feet to the ring of the sling. After a number of failed attempts, Charlie and I were convinced that it might be best for all involved to scrub our mission. Then ride participant John Crandell got out a polypropylene neck rope he had brought along "just in case" and, with deft ropecraft, quickly cast bowlines onto the sling and lift-strap D-rings. Soon a limp Goat was clearing the trees and swinging away for Heishman's Meadow, two miles north, to the jubilant cheers of all involved.

A minute and a half later, Goat was guided gently to the ground, and a sobbing but joyful Denise was hugging her beloved horse. An hour later, he was loaded and hauled 50 miles to Dr. Jeanne Waldron's clinic in Marshall, where his wounds were cleaned, treated and bandaged. The next day, he was trailered home to Upper Black Eddy, Pennsylvania, and Thursday he "tried to tear down the barn" to get out and romp. With a good bit of luck and the all-out efforts of an amazingly talented and caring group, Goat was resurrected from what could have been his rocky grave.

Matthew Mackay-Smith, DVM, has been the medical editor of EQUUS magazine since it was launched 20 years ago. An equine practitioner and horseman, he is a rich source of information and inspiration for those who create the magazine, as well as for those who read it each month. As for Goat, according to Matthew, "he went on to become a great endurance horse and a wonderful character, a marvelous horse to know and to be around."

Chapter 3

Forever Transformed

Coming Home

*How a determined escape-artist
mare changed the lives of two men one moonlit
night on the highway.*

DORIS DAVIDSON

Tip and Meg were cutting back. Not giving up the place, but cutting back on the work. They had leased the orchard and sold the cow. The hens had saved them the trouble of wondering what to do with them by dying of old age. Now there were only the two dogs and Tip's old mare, Trilby, to care for.

Tip was no rider, no cowboy, but he enjoyed a little ride around the neighborhood. Before he'd head out, he would fold a worn-thin Hudson Bay blanket on Trilby's hollow back, set on his father's old cavalry saddle, put on the old bridle with the fat snaffle bit and mount. Off they'd go, Trilby sashaying along, walking with the same enthusiasm she gave to grazing. "She's a walker, that one," Tip would say when he returned, a younger-looking man with color in his face.

"You always say that," Meg would reply, smiling.

"I can't help it," Tip would respond. "It's so."

It was the Nolans to the south who said they'd be happy to give the mare a good home. Tip and Meg both agreed to let her go.

"Do you think we did right?" Tip asked as they watched the trailer leave with Trilby inside.

"Ruth will be good to her," his wife said. "The kids will enjoy her. Her mane's better than a Barbie doll's hair to brush, and that's all their daughter seems to want to do. She'll get used to the new place. And anyway, throwing hay bales around doesn't do your arthritis any good."

In three days, the mare returned home. The Nolans said they thought that one of the children probably had left the gate unlatched.

Five months went by before Tip found the mare once more in the orchard, grazing in the desperate way ponies do. He liked to watch her graze, and didn't mention her return for two days. Talk about a selective feeder, he thought, as he watched her curl her upper lip around the different kinds of grasses. She never touched a weed, but wrapped her lip around the forage plants—the orchard grass, the white clover, the fescue and, oh joy, a clump of young alfalfa. Sometimes she would pause in the rush to fill her mouth to listen. Satisfied that the sound she heard was only the raucous bray of a cock pheasant, she would resume her quick chewing. Sometimes she would reject a clump of grass for no reason Tip could see. Something bitter? Tough? No matter, she would leave it, damp from her mouth, but not bitten off. Tip noticed, too, that she always left a part of the clump she was eating. Instinct, protecting next year's seed heads, he decided.

"She belongs here, you know," he said to his wife. "We shouldn't have given her away. One day she'll get killed running down the highway or getting through that maze of an industrial park."

And almost a year later, a similar conversation: "Do they want her back?"

"Yes, they say they do. John likes her and so do the kids. Even if she is an escape artist."

"Well, we'd better trailer her back. I thought when she went we were done with trailering."

"Perhaps, when she's really old and we've sold the orchard, we can get her back and she can graze on the lawn."

Tip never stopped thinking of the little palomino mare. Her image stayed with him like the dust motes that slid up and down his cornea. He'd see her drinking from the flume or drowsing in the sun, but mostly she'd be grazing. It was almost a year now since she'd come home.

There didn't seem to be enough to do since they'd leased the orchard. Meg tended her garden and kept herself busy in the community. One day, Tip decided he'd go to the fall fair in the community hall, partly out of a desire to get out and partly to buy an apple pie. Meg didn't much like cooking, and the ladies made good pies.

He parked the truck and walked through the hall—past the pumpkins, past the dried flowers, past the knitted booties and mitts and up to the bake table. He bought two pies and went out to put them on the floor of his truck before going back to enjoy a cup of coffee.

"Haven't seen you out riding for a long time, Mr. Leary." It was the young girl with the little Arabian.

"Getting too old. Gave her away."

"That's too bad. I bet you miss her."

"Yeah, I do. But I'm pretty stiff these days, and there aren't many good trails to ride anymore."

"That's no lie. Well, see you. I'm supposed to be helping."

Tip poured himself a cup of coffee, spotted an empty table and sat down.

"Mind if I share the table with you? Getting pretty crowded in here. Name's Bill," the man said, his big hand tipping back the other chair at Tip's table. "Heard your remark about no good places to ride," he said, sitting down. "You know, I had quite an experience a while back. Sure you don't mind me sharing the table?"

"Not at all," Tip answered.

Bill began his story. "It was night—between two and three o'clock. There was a lot of traffic, and I was hightailing it down the highway, when I spotted this horse running north. I could see it was pale like a ghost, its mane lifting and falling as it trotted on. We were both going the same direction, except it was on the left-hand side of the road and I was on the right."

"Keep telling," Tip said. "I've got to hear more. What color was this horse?"

"In the night," the man paused as he remembered, "it was sorta moon-colored. Moon crazy, too. Its head was up, and it was scared. Can't say as I blame it—cars coming at it from every direction, honking, lights blinding it. I made up my mind to pass it. Keep in mind I was driving a low bed, no weight on, but still a big rig. I gunned her good, got a ways ahead and pulled off on the shoulder. Had no rope, so I took off my shirt—lucky I've got long arms—and nipped across the road.

"It was really scary down on the highway. I was worried, too, that I'd spook the horse into the traffic—when it saw me, that is. There I stood on the upper side of the road, not much room between me and the hillside, peering south. There it was, galloping now, and kind of frantic—coming as fast as it could. It was the old and the new side by side, the cars and the horse, and, by golly, that night I'd have put my money on the horse. You ever see that picture of the black horse coming down the railway track?"

Tip nodded, his face tense.

"Well, that was nothing on this horse. It was all light—pale, moving light." Bill lingered on his last three words before saying, "Some kinda beauty, I tell you."

Tip leaned forward. "Yeah, I know what you mean, but go on telling."

"Well, on it come, galloping right up to where I was standing with my arms stuck out and my shirt hanging in the hand on the traffic side. As I said, I was scared to death this horse would veer into the traffic or spin around. But no, it stopped dead, and there I was crooning like a mother to a baby. Soft, real soft. It was breathing hard, soaked with sweat."

Tip had to ask. "Did it have a very hollow back?"

"Come to think, I guess it did."

Tip lifted his head. "That's Trilby. She was my horse, and by God, she'll be my horse again. She's 28 years old. What did you do next?"

"I kept makin' these noises. I was surprised, you see, because I'd never done anything like this before. Anyway, there she was in front of me. She smelled good too, like new-cut grass."

Tip smiled. "Yes, she would that."

"Well, I put my shirt around her neck, and I led her up the road, the direction we both were traveling. Must've walked three miles before I came to a field with a gate I could put her through. Along we went, this moon-colored horse wearing my shirt, and me, walking along this road. It was good to be outside. The air was moist, clean. The traffic died down too, and it was quiet, real quiet."

Tip looked around. He wanted to get out of there, but he had to hear the end of the man's story. "Go ahead, tell me what you did with the mare," he urged.

"I put her in this field. She tried to follow me. She'd have showed me where she lived if I could've left the truck that long."

"It was most of 10 miles," Tip said, "and she was back at the Nolans' place when they went out to milk the next morning. She wasn't gone more than 12 hours. They always phoned me when she got out because she'd come home to me. You see, they had given her away to a family 10 or so miles south of them. Didn't tell the wife and me. They'd sold an Appaloosa they had and threw in Trilby for free. She's some horse. I'm gonna bring her home. She can graze around."

"Yeah, she deserves that."

"Give me your address. I'll send you a picture."

"Thanks, but no. I'll remember her the way she was that night. What'd you say her name was?"

"Trilby."

"You know, that horse—she changed me. I look around a lot more now. Stop the truck now and then. Walk a bit. Look up at the sky, see the moon. Before it was car lights I was watching for. They bore into a person, those lights. Moonlight's different somehow. Yeah, you give that horse a good home. She's better than a course in stress management, that little homin' pigeon." The truck driver drained his cup and stood up.

Tip got up stiffly and held out his hand. "You ever need any help, you give me a call. Name's Tip Leary. We're on Leary Road."

Outside, Tip hurried to his truck. He'd go to the lumberyard first, get a few posts—treated ones. Then he'd stop at the farmers co-op for wire and staples. Maybe order a ton of hay. He'd rent a post pounder. Meg would phone the Nolans. In a couple of days, he'd have the fence up, be able to bring the little mare home.

Tip eased his shoulder back and forth. He could do it. Not so stiff that he couldn't hammer in a few staples.

Trilby could graze around. She'd be their pink flamingo on the lawn. He shifted the old truck into third gear, slapped the wheel hard and drove down the road, grinning like a maniac. He couldn't remember when he'd felt so good.

Captain's Last Lesson

A treasured companion succumbs to cancer,
but his legacy will last a lifetime.

VALERIA KILBY

The sun was shining brighter than it had a right to be on that August day in 1993. Too bright, in my mind, considering the devastating decision I had just been forced to make. After 16 years with my Welsh pony, Captain, I had slowly, numbly given my veterinarian the cue to give him the fatal injection.

Captain was suffering from cancer. In a space of 14 weeks, his condition had gone from the picture of a happy, healthy, hot pony to a dull, listless sack of skin and bone. I had suspected his condition for years, but other than several tumorlike cysts on the underside of his tail, he had never shown other signs of illness. My friend Dolly and I had wondered why it took more sweetfeed to keep weight on him than all the other horses combined. Early on, we simply labeled him as a "hard keeper" and left it at that. Once the cancer kicked in, though, we tried to fight it off for all those weeks. In the end, as almost always with this wicked sickness, we failed.

He was a yearling when I got him, full of himself and as aggressive as a stallion. I was just a kid, and my dad didn't really know what the previous owner meant when he called Captain a "proud-cut gelding." What we did know was that this unbroken black beast, with two white socks and striped hooves, was a giveaway in a package deal that included a very bombproof, kidproof, old pony mare. We left that day with two ponies in the trailer.

Two summers came and went, and the black youngster was now a dark dappled gray—and still hot to handle. We broke him to saddle and took him to the local horse show. His looks were right on. We placed in the halter classes. The rest of the day was a disaster, though; Captain made it clear that he was not the pleasure-pony type. He wanted to run.

Captain taught me that day to find his abilities and utilize them. In fact, throughout his life, he taught me a lot more than I ever taught him. From the start, his lessons were of responsibility, patience, friendship and trust. They were things I was in great need of. I was a short, fat kid who was extremely shy and had learned early on to avoid other kids, lest I be teased or, quite often, beaten up. I turned inward, and my closest friend became that gray pony. He was a friend I could talk to, who would listen, didn't care what I looked like or how fat I was. And he never ever made any moves to intentionally hurt me. We established a bond that didn't break.

Captain took me everywhere in the times that followed. I rode him on long summer days, during the few short hours between school and dinner, and on weekends. Weather didn't matter: We were always out. Together we discovered the world, wending our way down the back roads near my parents' house or chancing a run along the edge of a farmer's cornfield. We took in as many sights as we could before returning home by sundown.

Back then, our county still had a vast number of unpaved and untraveled dirt roads. Captain was always eager to go, and I was equally ready to oblige and turn him loose. He flew over the roads, running at a flat gallop, teaching me to love racing the wind and to enjoy the freedom and the unity that come from mutual understanding. We continued to go to local shows for fun. Halter classes were automatic—always in the ribbons—and I started barrel racing, pole bending and any other class in which the only competition was the clock.

Captain was barely 13 hands, but you couldn't tell him that. He taught me I could be a winner, no matter what my shortcomings might be. Captain got older, and his coat got whiter and whiter. Over time, I could no longer tell his socks without looking for the pink skin underneath. His mane and tail turned silver, and even the dark points along his muzzle, ears and legs faded until they disappeared. You would never have guessed from the way he acted that he was getting old, much less that he was getting sick.

Over time, I had grown up, graduated from pony to horse and let Captain settle into a more relaxed life at my parents' farm. I left for college, sold the horse, joined the Navy, went to sea, traveled all over Europe, Africa and southwest Asia, always seeking out some contact with horses. Through it all, though, I always returned home to Captain.

He was 16 by the time I got out of the service and came home for good. I began riding him again regularly, bareback. We took short trail rides because it was lost on me that he no longer was the sprightly youngster I once knew. He surprised me, showing his old speed and eagerness to go. It was as if he wanted to make up for the years we'd spent apart.

Captain turned 17 in the spring of '93. If someone had told me then that my pony would be gone before summer's end, I'd have called him crazy. Yet cancer is a fickle beast, with its own timetable and agenda. Watching Captain's sudden, steep decline was heart wrenching. We knew the fight was futile from the beginning, but as long as he did not appear to be in pain, we were going to fight it.

It didn't last long. When the time came, I couldn't make the call to the veterinarian; I had my mother do it for me. I was shattered, deluded into thinking that there was still something I could do to forestall the inevitable. But even as those thoughts raced through my head, I knew better. That morning, when I had gone out to feed him and check on him, I knew it was over. He came out to greet me, as he did every morning, but he was staggering, reeling like a drunkard. Thick drool hung from his lips, and for the first time I saw pain and resignation in his eyes. He had given up the fight. I sank to my knees before him, knowing that this was the beginning of the end.

Then it was over. Closing his lids over blank, staring eyes, I couldn't help but ask why I should lose my buddy this way. He was the pal I had grown up with, who had taught me everything I needed to know about dealing with life, including death.

Two Sisters

*How a lifetime's worth of experiences brought one woman
and a horse together forever.*

ELLIE PHAYER AS TOLD TO GERALDINE MELLON

I have a horse in Ireland. Truly, she's my horse. I've not bought her, but
we all know she's my horse. Sister is a 16.3-hand dark bay. I don't know
if she's the most beautiful horse in the world. I do know that never have
I had such telepathy with a horse. When I'm mounted, boundaries
dissolve. Horse and rider—sisters, if you will—share one body, one
mind and yes, one soul.

Sister and I met one misty Irish morning on the Connemara
coast, a day nearing the end of one of the legendary Willie Leahy's
cross-country rides. The previous evening a fellow rider had challenged
me to a race, come dawn. "A race it is in the morning then," agreed
Willie. That night, without my knowing, Willie sent 90 kilometers to his
stable for my special mount.

"You'll have Sister," he said next morning, and Sister stepped
out of the horse box into my life. Surprised, delighted, I quickly saddled
and mounted, eager for the prerace warm-up. Willie, in the meantime,
set off inspecting a mile and a half of beach to make sure the "track"
was safe.

From the beginning, Sister and I were of one mind. During the warm-up we connived, Sister and I. Sensing her power, I held her sharply in check. She immediately agreed with this strategy and obligingly relaxed, craftily hiding her true feelings and capabilities. Like two skilled poker players lurking behind a calm, almost lazy facade, we knew...we knew.

Warm-up over, Willie yet a distant pinpoint, we quietly watched the 20-odd riders stationing themselves along the course in gentle surf. Unexpectedly, my life began to flash before me. What a long way from the intellectual little Brooklyn girl, the girl whose musical talent led her to the brink of the concert stage. The young wife, mother and scholar turning to music of another sort, the lyrical magic of English and Irish literature. The young woman whose life lost its melody with the death of a beloved four-year-old daughter. Divorce. Teaching and single-parenting a son. Nervous years cured with self-doubt, grief, unnamed fear. And the son, nearly a man, gone to college.

Abruptly my thoughts returned to the race, and I gleefully anticipated flying with Sister, my Pegasus. Instantly catching the mood, she tensed, pricked ears in readiness. Not yet, Sister, not yet.

Retreating into the past, I recalled a certain horse ride, one of my first. The horse sped away at what I took for a dead gallop. Far from being frightened, I loved it and experienced total, absolute glee, the same emotion now dancing invisible pathways between Sister and me.

The "dead gallop" in my fortieth year pivoted my life, changing it forever. At age 41, alone, my uneasy world badly needing direction, I began riding. By the third lesson, I was jumping. I was making mistakes, but riding came naturally to me. From the time I started horse riding, free-floating nervousness plagued me no more. It simply disappeared. Riding competence sparked internal confidence, and fears receded into memory. Had it been eight years since my first lesson? Eight years leading me to the back of this gallant mare?

Sister stirred gently beneath me, nudging my thoughts toward the impending race. Still Willie had not returned from reconnoitering, and thoughts drifted again.

One year's riding, and I'm planning English riding holidays for college students, demanding—and getting, if you can believe it—the best riding instructors in England. By my second year, I knew I was great. That is no longer true, but in those days, I absolutely knew I was great. That second year, bent on impressing Maj. J.M.B. Birtwistle, trainer of English Olympians, I prepared to go over an indoor course of seven jumps.

"Ellie, the horse you're on stops at the fourth jump," warned an instructor.

"Not with me, he won't!" But, alas, the horse refused, while I, staying on course, cleared the jump with ease. Remounted, reluctant horse and red-faced rider cleared the jump in unison.

But something was wrong. Parts of that undergarment peculiar to women dangled near my wrists. What could I do? Heading for the next jump, I desperately tried to wiggle the offending garment into place.

"The hands," commented Maj. Birtwistle, "are very busy."

My antics undoubtedly fueled the cheeky American stereotype. Sister, I'm glad you didn't know me then.

Eight years in the saddle over hundreds of English and Irish miles and I became a weaver of dreams. My livelihood was accompanying riders to the British Isles. And to this windswept beach.

Today, Sister, the gods have blessed us, have granted us power to race the very wind. Confidence born of other lifetimes connects us. One in body, mind and spirit, we are invincible.

Suddenly, I understood that, as surely as we two were sisters and the race was ours, just as surely my life was mine, not to be lost to invading cancer. Weakened from chemotherapy, weary at the prospect of imminent surgery, I had arrived for this Connemara trek.

Willie, with uncanny Irish inkling, sensed the importance of this race, suspected the supernatural bond that would unite horse and rider. He felt it, and sent for Sister. Now joy coursed through my veins as her great body anticipated my thoughts.

The bets were in place, the markers laid, the spectators waiting, mounted in the shallow surf boundary. It was time. I licked salt spray from my lips, and we were off. I never felt her hooves cut into the sand; we were winged sisters racing our brother wind. It was no contest. The contender lagged 20 lengths when we flew across the finish line. We did it, Sister, we did it!

Later, I basked in adulation. Teenage girls braided my hair; fellow riders praised my skill. The race netted me 50 pounds, and Willie grinned, a knowing twinkle in his eye.

Still, the 50 pounds were a bit of an embarrassment. I had, after all, brought these riders to Ireland on holiday. Sister, the next day, continuing to read my thoughts, came up with the perfect solution. As we walked through a gap in a farmer's wall, a dry stone wall hundreds of years old, she cleverly arranged for me to bump my toe on a particular stone—the keystone of 14 feet of wall. Amid 30 stomping, wild-eyed, spooking horses, the wall, like so many dominoes, fell. When the dust settled, I handed my 50 pounds to the farmer.

And so the trek ended. I returned home and regained my health, as I knew I would. Two years have passed. We two remain sisters of spirit, often sharing misty green miles. Ireland shines as my special joy.

I have a horse in Ireland.

Like Ellie Phayer, Gerry Mellon began riding in her mid-30s. Ellie blossomed as a skilled dressage, jumping and cross-country enthusiast, while Gerry favored trail riding, hunter pace and horse treks. When Gerry briefly published a horse-trekking newsletter, the two women became friends over the phone but never met in person. Gerry describes Ellie, who died a few years ago, as having an indomitable spirit. At 60-something, Gerry "rides these days dreaming of Don Quixote."

A Teacher Named Kricket

A trusty school horse
helps a young woman find brightness even
during the bleakest of times.

Jeanne M. Rudmann

Everything in my life travels full circle; I have found that what is lost is regained, and people and animals who drift out of my life are sure to come back. Such was the case with Kricket, a nondescript grade gelding I first met when I was eight years old, who carried me through the worst times of my life.

Just before my eighth birthday, my mother was diagnosed with multiple sclerosis. By the time I turned eight, she had gone from the perfect homemaker to a depressed young woman waiting to die. My home life consisted of watching my mother first resort to a cane, later to a walker, finally to a wheelchair. The smell of urine permeated the house; screaming, threats and tears exploded, as my family flew apart under the stress of watching her decay.

To take my mind off our family problems, one day my aunt drove me to visit Carole Gerrity, her colleague and the coach of the equestrian team at Molloy College in Rockville Centre, New York. I'd loved horses since the day I was born, but because I lived on Long Island, I didn't step in my first manure pile until that day. Carole's horses were all beautiful to my starved eyes, but I was saving the best carrots for Billy, a white Quarter Horse with blue eyes. As I was feeding Billy, a sharp tug on my shoulder whirled me around and the carrots were snatched from my hand. Kricket introduced himself to me by dribbling orange spit on my arm and nickering triumphantly.

He was a large-boned, copper gelding of indeterminate breeding. The huge feet and feathered legs hinted at some plow-horse ancestry, but beyond that nothing was known. A woman had spied him standing in a field in the Hamptons while she was driving home from the beach. She had bought him on the spot and moved him to the stable owned by Carole and her partner, Linda Gillespie, where he lived the rest of his life.

That summer day, I rode Kricket. Carole hoisted me onto his back and led me around the ring while my beaming aunt snapped Polaroids. Thereafter, I slept with the black-and-white photographs under my pillow until they disintegrated. I named my horse models Kricket and begged to go back to Carole's stable, but no one could spare the time to drive me there.

By the time I was in my teens, my mother was in a wheelchair, could barely see and had been in and out of the hospital more times than I could count. Her friends had stopped dropping by, and her speech was so garbled that people who telephoned us thought she was drunk.

Once again, when things got really bad, I ended up at Carole's stable. Seven years had passed since the last time I was there, and I barely recognized Kricket in his winter hunter clip. But after only a few carrots, we were reacquainted. He was being used in lessons that afternoon, so I couldn't ride him, but I spent blissful minutes in his stall, grooming him and carefully combing out his coppery mane. That day I made a promise that somehow I would return, if he would only wait for me.

Three years later, I enrolled in Molloy College and joined the equestrian team, which Carole still coached. As I drove up to her barn and saw the familiar red buildings, I was shaking. Was Kricket still alive? To my relief, I spied him, bouncing a beginner around the ring on his bony, old back. He had been donated to Carole's school. By the end of my sophomore year, I had "adopted" Kricket by half-leasing him and working as a groom in Carole's barn.

Teacher and nurturer, Kricket cared for my emotional needs better than a human ever could. As my sophomore year rolled into my junior year, and my classmates talked of finals and dancing all night in Manhattan nightclubs, I was thinking about my mother; how she was unable to eat by herself, go to the bathroom or hold any kind of conversation. No one at home could spare the energy to listen or comfort me, but at the barn, with Kricket and my riding friends, I found nurturing. It was as if Kricket was saying, "I'll protect you. I remember who you really are, a little girl, not this sad human I'm carting around the ring every day." When I rode him he never faltered, spooked, bucked or took off, despite the many tales Carole's students shared with me over coffee in the tack room.

One November day, Kricket and I trailered with friends to a nature preserve for a morning's ride. I hadn't planned on going on the ride because I was afraid to be away from a telephone in case my family needed me. But Carole, Linda and my barn pals—Eileen, Janet and Kristine—convinced me to enjoy myself and go on the ride.

This was the first time I had ridden Kricket outside of a riding ring, and I was nervous as he picked his way down the sandy paths. But as the ride progressed, I forgot all about my problems, my fears, my angers. They were eased away in the scents of crushed pine and autumn loam. We burst into a clearing and through a meadow, then cantered through an alley of pines and cedars. Standing in my stirrups,

I turned my face to the bright blue sky and finally felt peace and acceptance of my mother's condition. I was flooded with joy—joy I thought I'd buried to protect myself from pain. It was as if Kricket was teaching me to accept emotions, good and bad. To this day, the scent of pine transports me to that eternal place where evergreens and bright celadon plumes caress the sky and Kricket eased me out of my pain.

The winter passed, and that spring Kricket was to accompany me in my showring debut, just as he had done with dozens of other students. Two weeks before the show, my mother died. The Saturday of her funeral was the only Saturday I didn't make it to the barn. The week after, while my family wandered through the house aimlessly, I stayed sane by preparing for the show. Scrubbing Kricket's mane, I scrubbed out my tears; polishing his bit, I wiped away years of illness and injury.

In the equitation class, the judge called, "All canter!" Kricket, normally a slowpoke, pricked up his ears and surged forward. At the end of the class, we lined up facing the gate and the ribbon winners were announced; Kricket and I had taken first place! I threw my arms around the old gelding's neck. I felt my mother's presence under that bright May sky. Somehow, I was sure, she had arranged the ribbon to brighten my memories of that May. She was never able to watch me ride while she was alive, but that day she was there.

Only after my grief for my mother was lessening did Kricket begin his own leave-taking. Two weeks before my college graduation and almost a year to the date after my mother died, we were jumping a cross rail when I felt his hind end crumple and collapse.

Kricket was euthanized on May 22, at the age of 28 or 29. I said my good-bye two days before. I didn't want him to know he was leaving me. I brought him carrots and groomed him meticulously, oiling his hooves, pulling his mane and trimming his chestnuts as if we were going to a show. We'd never so much as stepped out of the barn looking sloppy, and I wasn't about to let him leave that way. I will always remember Kricket as I left him, calmly chomping hay in his stall, watching through his narrow window as my car disappeared down the driveway, waiting for us to meet again. He taught me the beauty and joys of this world while all around me was ugliness. He showed me freedom under a November sky as we cantered through a meadow, a freedom I could never imagine while I felt trapped and helpless by illness and death. I know he'll never leave me, not now as I finally let go of those years of darkness and step fully into life.

Jeanne Rudmann, of Floral Park, New York, is a dressage and hunt-seat equitation enthusiast who trains and shows in both disciplines. She has counted herself a horseperson for more than 12 years.

Lost And Found

*For a brief time, a lost young man found solace
in the company of a hard-luck filly.*

LAURA HILLENBRAND

I have fingered over the contours of his face so many times in my
memory, back in that little corner where I keep my sorrows and regrets,
that I have caressed away the features. Only in rare moments, my face
pressed into a pillow, do I see it clearly. From her, I keep a black fistful
of mane, clipped from her withers a moment before she died. He was a
tormented refugee, who in his brief, wretched life took only the worst
from men and shed only light. She was a red dun filly, broad of back
and heart, once neglected, then adored, then mourned. I found and lost
them together.

I first met Allspice when I was a teenager attending a little riding
camp in Vermont, where she was my drill-team partner's mount.
Pressed into service at age two, Allspice spent her summer circling the
perimeters of a dusty ring with three dozen other horses whose names
changed with each summer's crop of girls. She had the watery coat and
gauzy eye of ill health, and she shouldered passengers with a profound
fatigue that was mistaken for sourness.

Assigned to evening water-pail duty, I came to know Allspice as
I bent over her half door, training a hose into her bucket and watching

her suck down its swirling contents. Leaning into her stall each night, I began to notice that her bedding always seemed to be drenched in urine, that starkly protruding ribs had sharpened her adolescent frame, that she stood all afternoon with her head in the back corner of her stall and drank gallons of water at a time, that other horses were so unnerved by her diseased proximity that they lashed out at her with hooves and teeth. I flagged down the stable director, but a call to her owner for permission to contact a veterinarian brought a stunning response: Forgo the veterinary care. He would sell her for slaughter and turn a tidy profit of $500.

My sister, Susan, and I searched for a way to save Allspice. My father's farm in Sharpsburg, Maryland, already populated with a semi-feral band of horses rescued from one ill fate or another, could easily feed another mouth. But in total assets Susan and I had only $200 cash, plus a $200 drum set our father had given us during a noisy childhood phase. The drums had to go, we decided, pooling our loot and offering $400 for the filly. (My father never knew the fate of the drum set. For several years he continued to ask how we were progressing on it, to which we would respond, "Great, Dad!")

The answer to our offer was no. But we would not be deterred. On the day the owner was to pick up Allspice, we rubbed handfuls of mud into her coat and left it to dry, making her appear even more haggard and pathetic than before. That evening, as the owner climbed from his trailer, my sister and I and several grooms attached ourselves to his extremities, pleading tearfully and even offering an extra $75 we knew we didn't have. Confronted by sobbing girls and a ghastly filly, he relented, driving away with a check for $400 and a promise of $75 more. We never sent it.

Susan swapped her entire summer's earnings as a camp counselor for Allspice's transport to Sharpsburg. The filly spent the first night shut in the backyard, away from the inquiring noses of the other horses. Susan and I camped out by the dining-room window to keep an eye on her. As the sun rose in the morning, Allspice spotted us through the glass and gently rubbed her muzzle on the pane to wake us. Then she trotted over to meet us when we padded across the lawn in our pajamas. From that hour forward, through care for the simply urinary infection that had been too much trouble for her previous owner to treat, she seemed to recognize that we had helped her and was, forever after, utterly smitten with all mankind.

In the weeks that followed, we watched the hollows of the filly's body become round with muscle, the dullness slowly leave her eyes. We learned that beneath the dull sediment of illness and neglect there was a horse who liked to chase cars down the driveway in greeting, who would climb on the front porch to nibble cornflakes, who would open the front door with her lips and walk into the dining room to say hello. She feared bicycles, bathtubs and small bodies of water. She had a tendency to plow directly through verticals, loved to feast on blossoms from my stepmother's flower garden and carried my family and friends with a gentleness that was almost tender.

Hussein was from Tehran, Iran, the son of royalty and privilege. When the Shah was overthrown and a bloody purge of the aristocracy began, Hussein's parents, to save his life, signed over their parental custody to a strange American man who whisked the teenager off to the United States just as the hostage crisis began. After dragging Hussein around the Northeast, the man came to Maryland, where he rented my father's farmhouse.

Dropped amid sparsely populated farmland in a country hostile to Iranians, Hussein was friendless, having lost his family and the interest of a caretaker who had become brutally abusive. He passed the whole of every day in loneliness, walking the fields nearby. At some point on one of those miserable days, he crossed paths with Allspice, and she, with her inexhaustible affection for people, began to walk with him.

Never having been near a horse, Hussein devoted himself to learning how to care for Allspice—what she liked to eat, where she liked to be scratched. Somewhere along the way, he heard the horseman's term "rubdown," and, using his limited English vocabulary, he interpreted it literally and liberally, exhausting roll after roll of paper towels to buff the filly from muzzle to tail. He never rode her, never even touched her with a stitch of tack, but they came to a private understanding; he would pick the burrs from her mane and wave the flies from her face, and she would walk with him, rub her face against his chest and ease his immeasurable sadness.

A year after Allspice's rescue, I arrived at the farm with a trailer to ferry her to a new home by the Potomac River, closer to my own. As we coaxed her up the ramp, Hussein emerged from the house and asked if we were taking her away. On that afternoon, we began what would become my dearest friendship. We spent hours with the horses, especially Allspice, and for a brief time, I believe, a small window opened in the smooth, featureless continuity of his grief.

Shortly before our final parting, on one of his visits to see Allspice, I slipped my helmet over his head and gave him a leg up onto her back for the first and only time. He pointed her head up the meadow and turned her loose; she sprinted, head low, eyes pinched to slits, ears flat, winging over the hill and out of sight. When I found them, they were standing by a gate, four long skid marks testifying to their precipitous stop. Unharmed, beaming and breathless, Hussein asked if he could do it again.

He slipped away over the winter. When his caretaker went months without paying his rent, my father had to evict them, and we slowly lost touch. New homes brought new isolation and loneliness, the desperate use of drugs furnished by his caretaker, crushing depression. One June day, Hussein laid down his heavy load; he picked up a handgun and performed the only act that could give him peace.

We lost Allspice the following month. Turning her out after a ride, I noticed her belly clenching and unclenching ominously. By the time a veterinarian arrived, the Potomac horse fever was entrenched. The filly lay in a puddle of mud with a fever of 107 degrees and agonizing laminitis while we poured water over her in a vain attempt to cool her. After three days of holding her head in my lap and squeezing water into her mouth with a sponge, I knew what had to be done. I pulled the halter from her head, clipped a wisp of mane from her neck and let her go.

In recent years, Laura Hillenbrand, a resident of Washington, D.C., has contributed numerous feature articles on a wide range of topics to EQUUS magazine. Laura is a Thoroughbred racing fan whose involvement with horses spans more than 23 years.

A Time To Heal

*A special Appaloosa colt helps a young woman
cope with a devastating loss.*

KAREN LEWIS GRANATH

My story begins with the familiar scenario of a girl whose shortage of funds was matched by an overabundance of love for horses. I lived for the times I managed to snatch a lesson here or a ride there, any style, any horse, any stable. Appaloosas were often my mounts, and their place in my heart grew as I came to appreciate how their unique color and versatility complemented their intelligence and humor. While I was in high school, my family moved to Warrenton, Virginia, and I finally realized my dream of having my own horse. My horse was, in his own way, quite a personality, although he lacked spots of any kind.

Boyfriends and college soon took up riding time, and my hunter was sold. My new dream was to marry the man I loved and have children, so my interest in horses was tucked away, occasionally satisfied by rides with friends. In May 1990, my new dream was fulfilled when I gave birth to a beautiful son. But soon my dream was shattered. Born with a very rare genetic illness, Ben died on his first birthday. In that short year, my role had changed from married careerperson with no children, to part-timer with one child, to full-time mother with a terminally ill child and full-time home nursing staff, to a wife, without career or son. My grief was compounded by a total loss of identity; I felt stripped of any direction and value. My husband and I struggled in our marriage as we faced major decisions about our relationship and the genetic implications of having more children.

After burying my son on a quiet hill in West Virginia, my parents, husband and I stopped by to meet Carol Petitto, then executive secretary of *The AraAppaloosa*, a registry publication. Before my pregnancy, Carol and I had become friends through the mail, when I saw an advertisement about her magazine. The publication was based in my mother's hometown. When Carol learned of our reason for being in her area, she insisted that we stop by to meet and share "horse hugs."

A very strange thing happened during that meeting. I numbly walked into Carol's pasture, followed by my dutiful husband, and felt the warmth of the sun on a spotted foal's neck. For a moment, I focused on nothing else. It was a simple act, but it was a miracle. That small touch sent me forward, to start healing. David, my husband, saw the act for what it was. I heard him question Carol about the cost and transportation of a foal to our area. To my horror, I realized that he was actually serious about buying a horse! Was this the same husband who had turned to me in grief just days ago, after adding up the mountains of medical and burial expenses?

Carol hugged us when we left and gave us a copy of *The Ara-Appaloosa* to occupy us on the long trip home. Mom and David tossed around the possibilities of buying a foal. I couldn't believe they were serious and kept interjecting doses of reality: "I don't know anything about raising a horse!" "What about all our bills?" "I don't have a job!" "I can't take on such a huge responsibility; I need time to recover from Ben."

But my all-knowing mother turned a deaf ear to my objections. "It'll work out, and here's your horse!" she said, waving a page from

The AraAppaloosa in front of me. My mother, whose experience with horses was limited to riding the plow horses on her grandfather's farm, had chosen a three-month-old foal in a farm advertisement. "This is the one," she said. "Just look at that spotted rump; there's an 'S' on it! Look at the way he's standing there—he knows he's special!" I argued in vain: "But Mom, he's a colt, and if I can't have any more children, I want a mare, so she can have babies for me." Now even I was entertaining the thought of having another horse in my life.

The ad also featured a beautiful filly, so a few days later, and with much encouragement from David, I called the breeder, Don Potter. I explained why I was calling and that we would be wasting his time, but I couldn't deny that his spotted horses—with their strong limbs, fine conformation and flowing manes and tails—had captured my fancy. Don could not have been more encouraging. As a parent, he said he couldn't imagine our grief. He invited us to "come out and see a real Appaloosa." He still had the filly in the ad, now a two-year-old, as well as the colt. We set a time, and off we went.

But when I got there, I hesitated before opening the car door. I didn't want to insult Don by wasting his time and didn't want to find something I liked but had no business buying with money that didn't exist. Steeling myself, I got out of the car. Don showed us around, explaining that his breeding is strictly along foundation lines, and his horses showed the Spanish influence preserved through numerous generations. As I looked at his horses, I knew I was looking at something rare and precious, just like my son.

Although the filly was gorgeous, she would mature smaller than what my five-foot, 10-inch frame required. I was disappointed, for she was exquisite. But I was glad that she would not work out, for this was really the only reasonable outcome, given our circumstances. Then David called to me to look at the colt that Mom had chosen for us the week before. As I turned, DJ's Repeat crow-hopped across his paddock. I asked Don if I could go in to touch him, and he told me to go ahead.

My presence in the paddock was met with reserved interest. "Peat" stood in a corner, facing me and watching intently. "It's okay, boy," Don said softly. Peat walked up, and in that moment I realized this was a horse who would boldly, yet intelligently, face a situation while listening to his rider. I realized something else, too: that the knowledge I'd accumulated about horses in my youth hadn't been forgotten. In fact, it was already sending me into a new future.

David asked if Peat was for sale. Don's answer confirmed the inevitable. I had no choice but to gather up my wits to accept a new challenge. I was encouraged that Peat was already trained to accept a bit and rider, so my job would be less overwhelming. Wait a minute! Was this really happening?

It really was, and it really did. I couldn't walk away from such a beautiful horse. I was equally scared and excited the day Peat arrived at our neighbor's barn. The ever-perceptive Don boosted his daughter onto Peat's back to confirm his great mind. I could not argue with a man who trusted his young daughter with his young horse.

From that confusing start through the first time I actually rode Peat, David and I learned how to communicate and regained our loving relationship. Peat taught us how to laugh again, as he met new challenges in sometimes unpredictable ways. On hard days, comparing notes on growth and just watching Peat eat and romp brought back the peace and joy so desperately missing from our lives. The money for his upkeep somehow always was there, as David and I worked together to provide Peat with a sound foundation for his life. We discovered that teaching a young horse is similar to teaching a child—limits must be set and rewards quickly given for a job well done.

Although I will never have memories of children growing up, Peat has provided some precious "childhood" memories of his own—such as the day he found an arrow from a summer-camp session in a field and proudly presented it to a horrified David, who was sure he'd been shot through the mouth. Another memorable incident occurred at a show, when a child ran up and attached himself to Peat's hind leg, taking him and everyone else by surprise. Peat picked up his leg, looked at David for help, then carefully placed foot and child safely on the ground. My farrier describes Peat as "a once-in-a-lifetime horse." The same strong, unique personality that drew people to my son is miraculously seen in Peat. Nurses fought over taking shifts with Ben; Peat gets the lone pat from the judge.

Today, Peat continues to heal our family with his beauty, personality and love of life. He is now five and loves to do anything I ask. David and I have a whole new world of friends and a great respect for life. Peat will, one day, dance for my son. Yes, he is a once-in-a-lifetime horse.

A dressage enthusiast, Karen Lewis Granath, who now lives in Chandler, Arizona, has been a horseperson for approximately 15 years.

"Peat is now seven years old and is, like my son, a true miracle. A 'real' Appaloosa, Peat is athletic, fiercely protective, intelligent and highly aware of his surroundings. His spirit soars in every task.

"Often Peat stands behind me while I sit awaiting our trainer. He tousles my hair, grins, eats both shirtsleeves and draws close to 'hug' me. Our relationship was not attained through luck. A greater hand put us together. I once had much taken from me, but now I have so much!"—Karen Lewis Granath

We'll Meet Again

*For almost three-quarters
of a century, Alice kept the memory of
Silver King alive in her heart.*

Robin Littlefield

My job was to handle Cassie, a small, fat Shetland pony. Her winter coat was so dense she resembled an English sheepdog, but Cassie had impeccable manners. Resolute and dignified, the little black mare moved slightly ahead of me as we approached the nursing home's electric doors. She set two stubby legs firmly on the rubber mat, and the doors swung open, as if announcing royalty. Cassie and I entered the nursing home.

It was uncomfortably warm inside, and the air was sluggish, laden with the stench of urine and disinfectant. Undeterred, Cassie marched forward, rounding the corner to the reception room. At least 20 chairs were arranged in a semicircle, and around it white heads bobbed like frosted balloons: some in half-sleep, others in immediate delight on seeing a shaggy pony.

Alice was pointed out to me, and I led Cassie through the oohs and aahs toward the wheelchair-bound, snowy-haired woman. It was Alice's ninety-second birthday, and Cassie was her surprise guest. With slender, bony fingers, Alice eagerly reached toward the pony's petite head. She caressed Cassie's nose appreciatively, cupping the tiny muzzle in her hand. In response, Cassie nuzzled her waxen palms.

"She's looking for carrots," the old woman giggled.

Kneeling beside the pony, I looked up into the near-century-old face. I was struck by Alice's beauty. Her bright blue eyes were reminiscent of summer skies on a cloudless day. She had pixie-cute features, a still-shapely mouth and powder-lucent skin: a noble face worn stately through many decades.

"You're a horsewoman?" Her eyes glistened.

"Yes."

"Yes, indeed." She nodded approvingly. "I can see it in your manner." Cassie rubbed her lips back and forth against the homemade lap robe.

"No carrots there, either," Alice grinned. One hand quickly followed the other as she repeatedly stroked the pony's neck. "I was a rider too, you know, when I was a young woman."

Having been told this previously, I nodded.

She spent several silent moments straightening Cassie's thick forelock. An attendant passed around small squares of white birthday cake. Alice and the pony no longer held the other patients' attention.

For a moment, Alice was silent. Then, with a faraway look in her eyes, she began to speak. "His name was Silver King," she said. "He was a big, gray Thoroughbred."

"Yes," I nodded, "tell me."

She paused, inhaled a deep breath. "It was more than 70 years ago, in Illinois, south of Chicago. The area was still quite rural then. I lived with my parents near a riding stable. And it was there I spent the best of my days."

She shifted slightly in the wheelchair, glancing down at me. Long, slender fingers seesawed through Cassie's mane, working the tangles free.

"And Silver King?" I encouraged.

Alice's face lit up. "He was beautiful. Full of life." She pointed her fingers inward and gently bounced them over her heart. "Such a vibrant spirit he had.

"There was a German trainer there. He rode all the horses. Big, heavy German horses. Mostly jumpers. And he did well with them, too, but he could never ride Silver King. Time and again he'd climb on him, start the training. Time and again Silver King would buck him off and jump the arena fence—saddle, bridle and all."

Her expression tense and stern, Alice stared at me as if reliving that oft-repeated scene. Her voice dropped, and she mouthed her words with a measured slowness. "He was too harsh with him.

"Others also tried to ride him. Always the same. Bucked them off, too. But I had befriended this horse, groomed him. I could see he was different. Wise and sensitive. I asked if I could ride him. I went slowly, carefully." She exhaled a deep breath and immediately rushed on. "He carried me everywhere—this proud Thoroughbred. For years I *listened* to him. And he taught me."

She tilted her head back, eyes traveling upward, a smile wriggling across her pale, lined face. "Often," she continued, "when people would see the big, gray horse coming, hear his hoofbeats as we galloped down the dirt road toward the big forest, people would say, 'Here comes Alice! Here comes Alice!'"

Her cheeks flushed pink. "We went there often. Silver King and I had a special place, deep in the forest—a small meadow where sunlight filtered through the trees. I'd take his bridle off. Turn him loose while I lay in the grass, my hands behind my head." Smiling, Alice paused to savor the memories of a life more than three-quarters of a century and half a continent away. "When you have a relationship like that with a special horse, nothing in a lifetime can compare."

For a brief moment, my thoughts traveled home to a 20-year partnership with the big, black Thoroughbred who for more than half of my life has always been there waiting for me.

Alice drew her gaze back to me. A sharpness slid over her nymph-like face. "In that day and age, women did not have as much voice in their own lives. When I was 20, my parents put me on a train bound for Hollywood. I didn't want to make movies. All the way west, rumbling along those tracks, all I thought about was Silver King.

"'What is he doing now?' I'd ask myself. 'Who cares for him?' I cried all the way to California."

She drew a deep breath. "Soon after I left, the trainer got back on him. Eventually Silver King again bucked him off, jumped the arena fence and took off, running down the dirt road saddle, bridle and all. They searched and searched, but never found him." Shaking her head, Alice stared at her folded hands. Her voice took on a colorless tone. "Fifty years later I went back. The stable was gone. The forest almost entirely cut down. They were covering it with a subdivision. I went to our secret meadow that had been deep in the forest, now freshly excavated. The construction workers told me they had dug up a skeleton. 'Musta' been a horse,' they said. 'Had a saddle and bridle with it.'"

Fighting back tears, I absently buried a hand in the pony's thick mane, slowly dividing the stiff, coarse strands between my fingers. For several moments Alice watched my fingers separating the sections of mane. In the silence, a thin, time-worn hand reached out and rested on top of mine. In unison, we slid our hands through the now tangle-free mane.

"He comes to me, you know."

She gently cupped her fingers through mine and held them stationary on top of the dozing pony's neck.

"Silver King comes."

I lifted my gaze and once again studied her face. The cloudless blue eyes never wavered.

"When I cross over, Silver King is there, waiting for me."

She watched my face, absorbing my reaction, and the tiny lines around her eyes softened. My lips moved, but no words came. Alice slowly shook her head from side to side. "No dreams, no meditations, sometimes for a few moments, I'm just there."

Alice enclosed my hands between her tissue-soft palms and drew them to her lap. I still knelt beside her wheelchair as Cassie quietly slept beside us. Alice looked down into my face and smiled warmly.

"My time is near, and I'm ready. Silver King is there, waiting for me."

CHAPTER 4

Chance Encounters

Heading For The Finish

*In the summer of 1936, all that mattered was preparing
a red-gold horse to race.*

ROSALIE MELLOR

Before I opened my eyes I knew it was first light. Lying still for a
moment, I heard the roosters crowing clear and far off before the earth
moved with the common sounds of day. In a dim and remote way I
gradually grew conscious of the faint smell of honey mixed with dust
in the low-hanging rafters. The aura of old comb and dead bees and the
ancient, inscrutable breath of the house itself hung in the room. Reaching for my clothes, I dressed quickly and silently crept to the door.

Down in the kitchen my father sat at the table, morning coffee
before him, hat cocked at just the right angle and shoes shined.
Although he was a horse trader, he never wore overalls or boots, but at
all times the dark suit and white shirt, dressed like someone going to an
office. He always had someone around to open the gates into the
muddy yards or to lead the horses out. Deep in thought this morning,
he was intent upon a neat pile of shavings heaped on the table like tiny
golden curls. It was his habit to whittle whenever he was figuring out
the details of a deal, a little pearl-handled knife held delicately in his
well-kept hands.

Setting forth with a few old nags, he had started trading horses when he was but a boy. No other work ever held any interest for him. He had tried road construction, running a meat market and working as a drayman, but sooner or later, he returned to horse trading. Horses were for him a touchstone, an axis upon which the meaning of life was hinged. Wherever he was or whomever he was with, he was figuring, scheming, talking horses. He remembered every detail of every trade he had ever made.

When I crept into the room, he looked up from his whittling and said, "'Morning, nice morning."

"'Morning," I mumbled, turning my back to find cereal and make toast over the glowing coals in the cookstove. As I buttered the toast, he poured himself another cup of coffee and sipped it slowly while I ate. After a long silence he remarked evenly, "The sorrel horse is looking good. He's picked up considerable since he had the sickness."

"Yes, he's getting fatter," I answered warily. It was difficult for me to talk to my father. I never really knew what he meant, for he was crafty and I was not.

"How are his feet holding up? I thought he seemed kind of ouchy the other day," he went on, looking hard at the growing pile of shavings.

"Oh, they're all right," I answered quickly, my voice taking on a nervous edge. "He is a little touchy walking on the cinders in the lane. I ride him along the side, though. And, of course, the track where I run him is dirt."

My discomfort grew as he persisted in talking about the horse I had been training all summer for the races. I didn't want to talk about Ginger to anyone, especially to my father. "I guess I'll go take him out before it gets too hot," I said and pushed my chair back so suddenly it tipped over. I felt the hot blood in my face as I bent over to right the chair. Glancing back, I saw my father was still whittling, focused on the orderly golden curls piling up on the table.

When I got out to the horses, the sun was behind them, casting shadows with long legs and heads in that strange early light. Dew sparkled in the grass, and the hens scratched and sang the way they do when they are looking for food.

Ginger stood under a tall tree along with the cranky spotted mare he was always with and Tom Thumb, the chestnut pony. The other horses turned toward me and crowded around, but they were just trading stock. Actually, they were all trading stock. Horses came and went every day.

Ginger nickered softly in recognition and came up to be scratched behind the ears, his warm breath sweet on my cheek. After brushing him thoroughly, I stood back to admire the way his red-gold coat caught the sun. How lovely he was, with his arched neck and the elegant set of his head and his happy, willing expression. He was never sour, and I knew even then that a horse like Ginger came once in a lifetime.

I vaulted up and, riding bareback, walked him down the lane slowly, the way you start horses out. The county-fair races would be coming up later in the summer, and I had been training for weeks, taking Ginger to the track every morning.

The air was magically cool and fair that morning, and there was no sound but the muffled clip-clop of the horse's hooves on the dusty road. Long shadows stretched across the way as we skirted the edge of town, taking a dirt road that wound around the park and led to the horse barns and the racetrack. As I drew near, I could smell the hay and manure and liniment and the aromas of leather and oil and of the horses themselves, lathered up with their workout.

Coming to my ears like music was the rhythmic cadence of hoof-beats muffled in the dust of the track, the measure of the trotters and pacers. Bright sulky wheels spun softly and the men clucked to their horses, voices low, "Easy, baby; steady, boy. Whoa now."

Jess was still working his gray around the oval, while Tom O'Brien cooled out the big black gelding who was blanketed and walking in the circle. Mr. Larson and Bill had both finished their workouts and stood along the fence to watch me warm Ginger up on the track. After I cantered him slowly along the outside, I lined him up and gave him a few starts, crouching low over the withers as he hit his stride. Mr. Larson took out his stopwatch, and the sunshine poured over the old men and their eager runners and one red-gold horse racing in the sweet morning air. As unattainable as I knew my wildest dreams seemed, nothing was impossible at the track early on a summer morning.

Later I rode home, and after giving Ginger a drink, I put him in the barn and went into the well house to quench my thirst. Then I went back to the barn to rub Ginger down. Spick, the hired man, was there, cleaning out the stalls. In spite of his periodic drunken sprees, when he would be gone for a week or more, he was a man invaluable to my father. He knew how to "cure" a horse of heaves, at least long enough to get it sold, and how to dye those gray hairs around a horse's muzzle so he would look younger than he actually was. Although he never appeared to like anything and went about his work swearing and grumbling, Spick was an artist at his job and knew all of the tricks of the horse-trading game.

He had his own ideas about grooming, and one of them was that the fetlocks should never be trimmed. I had tidied up Ginger's legs like the racehorses' the week before, when Spick was away on his binge, and now he noticed them for the first time. As I was brushing the horse down, Spick glared at Ginger's legs and then at me, his thin face growing more pale and pinched as he stared. "Who trimmed this horse's legs?" he snarled.

Halfway afraid of him, I stammered, "I did. All of the horses at the track...."

"I don't give a hang about them horses at the track. You just leave this horse's legs alone," he ordered as he stalked off, blowing snorts of smoke from his Bull Durham cigarette.

The summer rolled on from one hot day to another, and in August the county fairs and the brief racing season began. I rode Ginger in a few small races in the area, all the while looking ahead to the big race at the Humboldt County Fair where the King of Harts would be running. I could think of little else and woke up in the night with Ginger and the King of Harts running for the finish line neck and neck.

One anxiety nagged at me constantly. I did not have a proper saddle. Although I had been riding bareback in those small races, I knew that over at Humboldt I would be riding not against farm boys, but professional jockeys. I did have a respectable-looking bridle by this time, for I had traded for a racing bit, with its huge rings, and had fitted it up with short wide reins. Knowing there was no way I could ever beg, borrow or steal an expensive jockey saddle, I tried to forget about it.

One morning, a week before the race at Humboldt, I led Ginger around in the circle, cooling him out after his run. Mr. Larson came over carrying something behind him. I paused to see what he wanted and he drew out a little racing saddle, old and worn but polished so it gleamed darkly mellow in the sunlight. The girth had been replaced, and the stirrups shone like new. The old harness racer, talking out of the side of his mouth as he usually did so you could hardly understand him, mumbled, "Don't suppose you know anyone who could use this. I found it all dusty back in one of the barns."

Bill and some of the others gathered around, exchanging smiles like boys playing a prank. I glanced from one to another and then at the tiny saddle. My breath caught in my throat and I felt tears behind my eyes as I reached out one finger to touch it.

Mr. Larson thrust the saddle into my hands. "Take it," he said. "Some careless fool left it. You'll need this saddle next week over there at Humboldt when you run against the King of Harts."

Bill and Mr. Larson fitted the saddle on Ginger, shortening the stirrups with me up. They showed me how to sit and how to stand up over the horse's withers. All of the weathered old drivers gathered around to watch. "Don't he look a winner though," said Jess, his funny little smile wrinkling his face. Lining up at the rail, they cheered as I galloped Ginger around the track, turning on a burst of speed in the homestretch.

Riding home I took the long way through town and passed the sale barn where horsemen hung out. I tried to look indifferent as if I had ridden in a racing saddle all my life. Each morning, when I took Ginger to the track, I fitted the magic saddle on him and imagined him running against the King of Harts. In my reverie, he always won by a nose.

One afternoon a few days before the big race, I went to the granary and took Ginger's bridle from the hook. Spick stood just inside the door, rolling a cigarette with great care, licking the edge of it and twisting the end. Knowing he had something to say, I waited, holding the bridle as he fumbled for a match, scratched it on the seat of his striped overalls and cupped his hands around it as the small light leaped toward the cigarette. The thin bitter face was colorless and the mouth holding the smoke tight and unsmiling.

Inhaling deeply, he turned toward me, but his flat gray eyes studied something just above my head. He pushed his sweat-stained straw hat back from his forehead and said at last, "If you're fixin' to get that sorrel horse, he's gone. Left in a truck this morning when you wasn't here."

I felt the blood leap to my face and then drain away. Everything spun around for a few seconds, and I leaned against the wall and bit my lower lip, not daring to look up. My grip tightened on the bridle and I fought back tears. Not for anything would I have Spick see me cry.

He was bent over the tack box, and it took him a long time to find the brush he wanted. When he straightened up, he said, "Your dad only paid $40 for that horse, thin as he was and sick with shipping fever. He sold him for $60. That's a good profit. Times is hard, you know."

I knew how hard times were—that Spick worked hard for a dollar a day, and many men had no work at all. "He'll have a good home," he went on. "A feller from Fort Dodge bought him for his boy."

He started to leave then but hesitated and looked back at me, a frozen little figure still clutching Ginger's bridle. "Besides," he added, "what's so special about that horse anyway? He's only a horse, has his faults same as any of them."

I hung the bridle up beside the little saddle, and for a long time they gathered dust. The next morning I looked out to the pasture where the horses grazed and saw the cranky spotted mare and Tom Thumb and the others, but Ginger was not among them.

The King of Harts broke his cannon bone in that race at Humboldt the next week and had to be put down. The summer, with its heat and wind and terrible dust storms from Dakota, drew to a close, and fall came. Geese flew south and the pond froze and it snowed. The wind blew and the sun came up and went down, and the same stars shone in the sky night after night. The next spring, green crept from the willows to the grass and at last to the other trees, and birds built nests again.

That summer when I awoke early I heard the cool sound of pigeons in the eaves and, far off, the roosters crowing. My thoughts went to those other mornings when I had ridden Ginger to the track, and I told myself Spick had been right. Ginger was only a horse and had his faults just like any of them. I would have a better horse than him someday.

But I never did. There were other horses. Later I owned a lovely bay, three-gaited Saddlebred mare who, one spring day, threw me off right in front of the sale barn but settled down and went on to win many shows. There was the fun-loving Rhett Butler I raised from a colt and the five-gaited palomino, The Sheik, who would rack on as he came down Main Street, with men stopping their cars to watch as the beat of his hooves rang out, "A peck, a peck, a half a peck."

There were always horses, but there was never another horse like Ginger, a red-gold horse with an old racehorse man holding the stopwatch on him as he ran around the track early on a summer morning, his delicate little hooves leaving prints of gold on a track that stretched forever to the sun.

The Rockefellers Owe Me $2

*A brief encounter on a long-ago summer day leaves
a young rider with an unusual unpaid debt.*

THOMAS F. SCAMMON

I was 14 years old and living on Mount Desert Island, off the coast of
Maine, when I first encountered the Rockefellers. As everyone knows,
that large island has long been the summer home for hundreds of
millionaires, always referred to as "rusticators" by the native residents.
From an early age, we were taught that rusticators were an odd lot, and
if they sometimes asked foolish questions, we must always be polite
and patient with them.

In the summer of 1930, I was working on Heman Rodick's farm,
located near the end of Eagle Lake and not far from a network of
carriage roads owned and maintained by the Rockefeller family. These
roads, open to the public, were for horses only. One morning Heman
and I went down to New Mills meadow to cut a load of green hay for
the livestock on his farm. After the hay was cut and loaded, Heman
took the rake home and left me with the workhorses and the wagon
load of hay.

Now Heman had set off on a paved road that led up to a steep
hill, but I decided on a different route that would be easier on the
horses. This was the Rockefeller road, which was freshly graveled and

raked. I was unconcerned that the iron wheels of the heavily loaded wagon would dig deep into the gravel or that the shoes of Heman's freshly shod horses would make pronounced holes at every step. In fact, it pleased me to look behind and see the straight lines made by the wheels and the perfect spacing of the horses' hooves.

On that beautiful, cloudless day, I was happy as a lark and looking forward to Heman's bountiful supper table after a day in the fields. Suddenly, I heard a voice shouting angrily at me. Turning, I saw a man and a boy in a buggy. A quick look at the boy's clothing told me that he was a rusticator. Thinking that the shouting man wanted me to get out of the center of the road, I pulled the team to the side to allow the buggy to pass. But as it came alongside, I realized the driver was incensed by my messing up the smoothly raked road. It was then that I recognized him as the foreman for the Rockefeller estate.

When he started brandishing his buggy whip, I was fortunately far out of his reach, but since one good turn deserves another, I reached for a long-handled pitchfork stuck in the load of hay. Perhaps deciding that discretion was called for, the foreman drove on, first promising to take this up with a higher authority—that is, my employer. This threat bothered me not at all, for Heman cared no more about the Rockefellers' gravel than he did about a cow path.

The rest of the trip home was uneventful, but this incident was to cost me $2.

At this time Heman was renting part of his big barn to a man named Mr. James, who ran a riding school for the rusticators and also bought and sold horses. When I had a bit of free time from farm work, I sometimes worked for him. The very next morning after my encounter with the foreman, Mr. James, having just sold a big dappled-gray mare named Sparkles to the Rockefellers, asked me to deliver her to the family's stables. A groom would be there to receive the horse and to pay me $2 for my work, and Mr. James would retrieve me and the saddle and bridle with his car.

As I mounted Sparkles, I was cautioned not to get the mare over-heated, and to this I readily agreed. But Sparkles had stood in her stall for three days, and no one had thought to cut down on the heavy feed of oats regularly given Mr. James' horses when they were working. Always a high-spirited animal, the mare was now so full of energy that she wanted to burn some up. In short, she wanted to run flat out, and the snaffle bit in her mouth was hardly the best thing to restrain her.

As she approached the carriage road, only a short distance from the barn, she became almost uncontrollable. Then she began jigging and going sideways down the road. When we almost went into a ditch, I was so fearful lest she hurt herself that I gave some slack to the reins, in the hope that she would straighten out. Given the opportunity, she did. Bolting, she took off on a dead run—I had totally lost control.

Sparkles ran nearly the length of Eagle Lake before I could slow her to a canter, and we were approaching Jordan Pond before I could bring her to a walk. A dappled gray when we started, she was now white with foam. I dismounted at the top of a grade and tried to cool her off by rubbing her down with grass and leaves. When she grew calmer, I decided to go on to the Rockefeller stables. But my hopes were short-lived, for Sparkles still wanted to run, and, running, she started to sweat again.

Arriving at the stables, I expected to find a groom to receive the mare and to provide my anxiously earned $2. What I found instead was the whole Rockefeller clan and their friends assembled. Worse still, there was the foreman I had encountered the day before. Seeing me again and noting Sparkles' lathery condition, he started toward me in an angry, threatening way. I quickly dismounted, stripped off the bridle and saddle and put them and myself into Mr. James' waiting station wagon. Impatient to be off, Mr. James lost no time in getting started, and we rode back to the farm in total silence. It comforted me a little to suppose that when Heman got the chance, he would collect the $2 for me.

He never did. Nor did I. I moved on to other bigger things—the Depression, World War II and earning a living. Like most Maine men, I have seen good days and bad, but I have always taken pleasure in an experience not enjoyed by many: The Rockefellers owe me $2.

The Fastest Horse
On Four Hooves

*Keeping up with a homely, aging speedster named
Mr. Clean was a difficult, but rewarding, proposition.*

MARCIA L. HOUSE

I first met Mr. Clean when my boss unloaded him from the trailer at the public riding stable where I worked. Newly saved from the dog-food man at the local auction, the flea-bitten gray horse shot out of the back of the rig, nearly dragging her out with him, and stood blinking in the late afternoon sun.

"He's certainly homely," was my first thought. He was skinny, with a telltale, bad-case-of-worms potbelly. His coat looked as if no one had groomed him in at least a year, and he had a deeply dished face, although he obviously had no Arabian bones anywhere in his body. He also was old—further examination showed him to be at least 20. His only attractive feature was the wise and knowing look in his eyes.

"Oh boy," I thought, "the boss felt sorry for another one," and I shook my head as I led him off to his stall. Later that evening, the new arrival was christened "Mr. Clean" by the staff—a joke because the horse was anything but, and also because the look in his eyes reminded us of the character on the detergent bottle.

We soon found out, however, that we should have called the old guy "Whoa Boy." Once Clean was dewormed, fed and cleaned up, he began to feel better and he became the fastest thing on four feet. We rode him in a snaffle; we rode him in a pelham; we rode him in a Western curb, but the result was the same. As soon as Clean left the stable yard, he was off like a shot and nothing could slow him down. Fortunately, he was also careful, and he jumped high and clean, always choosing just the right spot for takeoff. Once we got used to the speed at which he jumped (and thus stopped getting left behind), it became great fun to ride him around our little cross-country course, feeling a hurricane of wind in our faces and watching the blur of trees as they whizzed by.

Clean's speed, however, posed one significant problem. Very few people could ride him. All but our most advanced students were terrified of him, and most of our rental customers would have been killed if they took him out, frightened to death by his sheer velocity even if they managed to stay on. So Clean stood around a good bit of the time, but he soon found another way to make himself useful. Because he seemed content in his new home and never wandered away, we left him loose in the yard and he became our official greeter, sauntering up to people as they got out of their cars and offering a friendly sniff. New customers were often startled when Clean walked up to their cars and stuck his head through an open window to check them out.

He also became the overseer of our "maternity ward." He quietly took charge of our small broodmare band, making sure that the mares, and later their foals, stayed out of trouble. At feeding time, he would stroll through the gate, round up his charges and herd them in. He even licked and groomed the foals, and the mares never seemed to mind. It was almost as if the wise look in his eyes and his benevolent manner communicated to our equine mothers that all was well as long as he was in charge. When three of the working students bought an

$18 orphaned pony foal at auction, Clean became the little one's surrogate mother, looking out for the youngster with the efficiency and concern of the best mare and watching closely as we bottle-fed the baby. Soon the foal followed Clean around the way the other foals followed their dams. It was quite a sight to see our three mares in the pasture with their babies and Clean carefully keeping watch over his own foal.

In the two years that I knew Mr. Clean, only two riders ever showed up who could handle him. One, an advanced student, eventually bought Clean but continued to board him with us, allowing us to use him as we had before. The other, a cowboy from Wyoming, came out every week to ride him. Dressed in Stetson hat, expensive boots and silver belt buckle, he would head off into the field with Clean totally content and under control. We even saw the man teach Clean some simple reining patterns, which he performed with admirable precision.

Of course, there were others who ventured to take on our aging speedster. One Saturday morning, for instance, a young man called to make reservations for a trail ride with some friends. He told us that it was his birthday, his friends had promised him a trail ride as a present, and he wanted the fastest horse we had. "We have a fast horse, all right," I said. "Are you sure you can handle him? Are you really, absolutely sure?"

"Oh, yes," the young man replied, obviously excited. "Just put a Western saddle on him, and I'll be there."

"You'd better go out with them to make sure this guy doesn't get into trouble," said my boss when I hung up the phone. "And make sure he signs a release," she added, echoing my thoughts on the matter.

The birthday boy and his party arrived on schedule later that day, climbed up on their horses, and together we headed out. But as soon as we passed through the gate into the field, Clean took off. With one hand his rider hung onto the saddle horn for dear life, and with the other he waved his cowboy hat, shouting "Yaaa-hooo" as he disappeared over the hill. Several minutes later, we heard hoofbeats approaching us from behind. Clean swept by the ride at his usual breakneck speed, his rider still hanging on, waving his hat and shouting "Yaaa-hooo" at the top of his voice as they once again disappeared from sight.

Over the next half hour, Clean passed the ride five more times, and twice we saw him and his rider from the top of a hill. Then, five minutes passed, 10 minutes passed, and we didn't see them. I was starting to get worried, when I saw Mr. Clean explode out of the woods and head for the barn, minus rider and saddle. "Oh, no," I thought, and ordered the ride to dismount and hold their horses before I took off in the direction of the woods. As I approached, I saw the birthday boy emerge from the trees, saddle under his arm and a big grin on his face. "Cinch broke," he laughed. "Boy, did I have fun!"

Two months later, I left the farm for a teaching job at another barn. A few days after my departure, I received a frantic phone call at work from my former boss' son. "Clean's down in the field," he cried. "My mom's not here, I can't reach his owner, he's breathing hard, his eyes are glassy, I think he's dying. I called the vet. He's on his way. What else can I do? Can you come?"

With a quick explanation to my new employer, I jumped in my car and raced to the farm. But by the time the veterinarian and I arrived, Mr. Clean was gone. "What killed him?" asked the boss' son between sniffles. "Old age, son," the veterinarian replied. "He finally ran out of gas."

We had always joked that Clean moved so fast because he realized he didn't have much time left and he wanted to pack as much into it as he could. When he passed away at age 20 (plus who knows how much more), we all knew we had lost a good and wonderful friend.

Clean's owner had him buried on the farm, out in the fields he loved. The cowboy from Wyoming, who had introduced Clean to reining, came out to the farm and cried.

In nearly 20 years of working with horses, I have never met another horse like him, and I'm grateful I had the chance to know him. I'll never forget speedy, wise-eyed Mr. Clean.

Reborn To Run

Who would have guessed that just a month of patient training and tender loving care would finally enable a little mare called Regal Rachel to live up to her name?

JO STEBER DUFTON

To this day, I want to believe she ran just for me, that homely Thoroughbred mare who bore the unlikely name of Regal Rachel. I remember the day we claimed her; I groaned when the decision came down that she was to be in my care. As a groom on the racetrack, you vie with your peers for a string of runners, horses that will earn you stakes and recognition in addition to your weekly salary. Rachel looked anything but regal, with her dull, shaggy coat and ill-proportioned body. All she'd earn for me, I was sure, would be chuckles and snorts from every other groom under the shed row.

Rachel was a small mare, just over 15 hands tall, and the prominent ribs that poked out from her barrel attested to the poor condition of her teeth. Lord only knew how long it had been since she'd been able to eat comfortably. The first order of business was to float and level her teeth, then begin a diet of oats, sweetfeed, warm bran mashes and as much hay as she could eat. She also received a special regimen of vitamins, along with a full body clip, to promote the growth of a new, healthier coat of hair.

For two weeks, Rachel did nothing but walk and eat. A racehorse's mental state is as crucial to performance as her physical conditioning, and this mare's attitude was one of absolute defeat. She had been battling not only other horses but her own body's deterioration for so long that she had nothing left to give. Yet she retained a sweet nature and responded gratefully to every kindness shown her.

Mornings are a lively time around a racing stable. The backstretch bustles with grooms preparing their charges for workouts, exercise riders waiting to mount up and hot walkers cooling out horses after brisk morning gallops. Rachel watched the activity with growing interest and developed a habit of pawing at the mat in front of her stall when she wanted to join in the fun.

Instead of handing Rachel off to someone else for her daily exercise, I walked the mare myself, taking her on long, relaxing tours of the backside stable area. We would explore the field behind our barn, taking time to graze and watch as other horses were being washed and watered off. We often ambled past the track, and her ears would stand at attention when horses thundered by, dueling for the lead in workouts designed to bring out their competitive edge. Her nostrils would twitch as if she could smell the excitement of the contest. Her eyes would follow them out of sight. I found my hopes rising: This mare wanted to run.

We began a training regimen of light pony work. Wearing only a halter and shank, Rachel spent her mornings jogging alongside our stable pony, Oliver, a huge Appaloosa gelding. Together, they would jog the wrong way around the track along the outside rail, maintaining a steady pace that would serve as the foundation of Rachel's training. Little by little, the mare's stamina increased, her muscle tone improved and her attitude underwent a delightful transformation. Where once she had hung her head and literally plodded on her way to the track, she now arched her neck in anticipation of a spirited romp and danced in place while waiting her turn to begin.

The time came for her workouts to be lengthened into one-mile jogs, which were followed by another mile of galloping the "right way" on the track. She moved strongly by now, pulling the old Appaloosa along with her, and each day she seemed more eager to return to the role for which she was bred.

Thirty days had come and gone, which meant Rachel was "out of jail" as far as having to run back at a price higher than that for which she was claimed. However, she was coming into form at a level beyond her previous $3,500 price tag. The decision was made to enter her in a $5,000 claiming race and see how she fared. She hadn't had a rider on her back in six weeks, and we figured this race to be little more than a workout. Come to find out, Regal Rachel figured otherwise!

Going six furlongs, she broke from the gate slowly, falling in behind the field of eight other horses. I watched her tail and ears for signs of discontent, but none was evident. She was running within herself, steady and strong. As the field entered the turn, she moved up to challenge the fifth- and sixth-place horses. Coming out of the turn, she nosed into fourth and set her sights on the front-runners.

We watched with barely controlled excitement as Rachel bore down in the stretch, sending herself into overdrive. She captured third place, then pulled into second with another stride. And suddenly she was vying for the lead! Rachel and the other horse ran side by side, and as they flashed under the wire, the finish was too close to call.

All eyes were on the tote board, where the photo-finish sign was blinking. We held our breath as the minutes passed, waiting for the track stewards to review the race's finish to determine the winner. We were ecstatic when, suddenly, Rachel's number lit up the first-place box. The little mare had run a hell of a race, coming from off the pace to nail the win by a nose.

Rachel's sides were heaving when she pulled up in front of the stands, and sweat had darkened the hair around her eyes, making her look all the more exhausted. We made the victory trip to the detention barn for urine testing, then headed back to Barn 24 for cooling out.

I was proud of the way she'd run. Rachel walked placidly beside me, carrying herself in a quiet, dignified way as if to tell me that she, too, was satisfied with a job well done. I let her graze until she was completely cool, then put her in her stall and massaged the muscles in her back and shoulders with a cooling brace. I rinsed her legs with alcohol and bandaged them up, then packed her feet in mud to draw out any heat or soreness that might linger after such a strenuous afternoon.

Regal Rachel continued to train well, and two weeks later she ran seven furlongs for a claiming price of $8,500. Posting her second win in as many races since coming into my care, the mare ran as she had the time before, making a big move from off the pace to catch the leaders in a stretch drive.

Rachel's performances were beginning to pique the interest of a number of trainers, and I realized that it was only a matter of time before someone else would want to own the little horse I had grown to love. That's the nature of the claiming game: All horses in claiming races are for sale at the specified price, and to buy one a trainer need only to put in a "claim slip" before the race stating his intent. A horse like Rachel, whose form was improving, is an especially enticing claim.

My only consolation was that if we continued to run Rachel for increasingly higher claiming prices, prospective buyers might wait to see where she leveled off. That way they could be sure they were investing wisely.

Rachel's next race was for a claiming price of $10,500, three times what we'd paid for her in the spring. She was the picture of health, prancing into the paddock for saddling, her sleek bay coat shining with vitality. Her legs were tight and sound, and the rundown bandages on her hind legs were only a precaution. She was a tempting prospect to anyone with half an eye for claimers.

I led her onto the track, handing her off to the lead pony and stepping back to admire the change I had helped bring about. She made a striking picture, head held high and ears alert to every nuance of the world around her. I watched from the rail as she went into the gate like a champ. She broke slowly, as always, but began her familiar assault on the horses in front of her as soon as she settled into stride. I felt my heart swell with pride as she boldly moved between horses, saving ground along the inside. She was eating them up alive. The crowd had bet her down to second favorite, still not convinced that she had what it took to put away the number-four horse, a high-priced claimer running in cheaper company for the first time.

But Regal Rachel didn't run by the numbers, didn't adhere to the expert opinions in the *Daily Racing Form*. She ran on heart, pure and simple. She steadily made her way past horse after horse until only one remained in front of her. The roar of the crowd reached a frenzied crescendo as Rachel set her sights on the favorite. Each stride brought her closer to victory. My own voice joined in the chant of the people around me: "Go, baby! Go, baby!"

She pulled a final burst of speed from somewhere deep inside her and thundered past the grandstand a full length in front of the favorite, clinching her third victory in an impressive, decisive manner. As I ran out onto the track to pick her up, the paddock judge met me with an apologetic expression.

"Jo, she's been claimed. Bring her back to the paddock, please," he said.

The joy of Rachel's victory suddenly turned to a dull, heavy ache in the center of my chest. I held her while the jockey pulled off the saddle and pad, then walked her slowly back into the paddock where another groom stood waiting with halter and shank to take her to a new barn, new trainer, new owners. She stood docilely while her life changed hands, and I gave her a parting embrace as they led her out into the light.

My ego made me want to believe she ran for me, out of gratitude for all that I had done to bring her to this place of sweet success. As I watched her walk back onto the track, her head raised and her eyes sweeping the stretch for the sign of yet another challenge left unmet, I realized she now ran for a reason far more important—she ran for herself. Regal Rachel had become all that her name implied.

The Windfall Horse

Apples was old and wise, and although he stayed only a short time, he left a lasting impression.

MARY HARRISON

The first horse I ever had wasn't really mine. It was in September, 27 years ago, that Arthur came stomping across our plank porch and thrust his head in the cabin door. Arthur was our neighbor, landlord and friend.

"I got a hoss. Guess it's a hoss. Looks more like an elephant to me."

"Where?" I unplugged the washing machine, grabbed Al's jacket (it wouldn't close over my pregnant belly), swung Mandy to my hip and went out the door.

There was a small sawmill just beyond our log cabin. One shed, at the top of a rise, was no longer used. Arthur was heading for that.

"Those two fellers said they couldn't cut pulp wood for me without a hoss. So I told 'em to go to Bangor and get one. This is what they come back with." Arthur grumbled, yanking open the door of the old shed. It was dark inside, but it certainly smelled like a horse.

He was 17 hands high. His feet were like buckets, and his legs were like telephone poles. His swayback said he was old; so did his loose lower lip and the hollows over his eyes. As I got used to the dimness, I could see he was strawberry roan with a wide blaze. His mane was worn where the collar had rested on it, and his shoulders were scarred from old galls. Mandy cooed and patted his neck. He whuffed softly at her. She struggled to get down, but I didn't trust him that much. I backed out of the stall. After that, whenever I got feeling housebound, I would take Mandy and slip into the woods to watch the old horse work. I called him Apples, for he was the color of the windfalls outside our cabin door.

He knew considerably more about logging than did the two men who drove him. Often they tried to put him places where the logs he was chained to would get hopelessly snagged. They would yell at him and hit him with the reins and with branches. Once I caught one man beating him with the blunt edge of the ax. The horse would stand there, legs stubbornly braced, head down. After a while, the men would give up and walk away.

As soon as he was left alone, Apples would turn his head and look things over. Then he'd back up a little and edge sideways, maneuvering back and forth until he got those logs untangled. Then he'd twitch them out his own way, slick as you please.

More than once, when he was thirsty, I saw him search out a damp, soggy place. He'd paw with that huge hoof until he had a good-size depression, which would fill up with water. Then he'd drink it dry, move on a little and paw out another.

He had reason to be thirsty. I would go up to the mill shed now and then after supper just to visit. That's how I found out the pulp cutters often put him away still hot and without water. After that, I slipped up every night, curried him and led him down to a spring near our cabin to drink.

One night I led him over by an old flatbed truck in the mill yard, climbed on the truck and slipped onto his back. From then on, I rode him every night to water until Al caught me and, horrified, made me promise to stop.

I cleaned out his stall, too, until I got too pregnant to shovel. I made so much of old Apples, it got to be a joke. Al and Arthur teased me constantly.

Halloween was dark and rainy. The pulp cutters came just before supper. The mill yard was all mud, and their truck was stuck. They'd hitched the horse to it, but he had fallen and wouldn't get up. Would I try? After all, he liked me.

I saw Al's headlights pulling in so I sent them to get Arthur. I kissed Al welcome home as I struggled into my raincoat, told him over my shoulder to turn off the oven and mind Mandy; I'd be right back.

The truck was in mud to its running boards.

Apples whinnied as I came through the rain. He seldom whinnied. He'd been down so long that the side he was lying on was numb, and he couldn't get up. I held his head and swore.

Soon Arthur backed his car into the mill yard. I watched helplessly as they chained the horse to the car and dragged him forward, free of the truck and the slab pile. Quickly they wrapped ropes around his legs and pulled him over onto his other side. He got up at once.

Apples was up, but the truck was still stuck—and, by now, so was Arthur's car. I led the trembling horse to his stall and gave him hay. I couldn't manage the harness, so I went back to the cabin. Al went up to tend the horse and help unstick everyone. I never did find out how they all got out.

Al had gotten a good look that night at the shed where Apples was kept, so the next weekend he bought a roll of tar paper and covered the shed to stop the worst of the drafts.

Not long after that, we were awakened at two or so in the morning—I was too sleepy to be sure of the time—by a loud, rhythmic thumping on the porch. Terrified, I clutched Al, who was having a hard time disengaging the bedclothes as it was. He finally struggled free of them and of me, and crept to the door. By this time, the thumping had given way to a most peculiar scratching.

Al flipped on the light and threw open the door at the same time. There was Apples, blinking stupidly in the sudden glare, his great head thrust into our living room, shoulders pressing against the doorway.

Al pulled on his clothes, got the flashlight and led the old horse back to his stall. He came down again for a hammer and nails. Apples had simply walked through the front of the shed. The second time it happened, we left the shed door open so he could come and go as he pleased. It was too much trouble nailing things back. When it got quite cold, we tied him at night to keep him in.

It didn't get cold early that year, though. I remember the first snow, and Apples coming in from the woods, bells jingling on his harness, black mane all frosted, breath clouds puffing from his nostrils, snow arching in a great spray from the dragging logs. But the snow was light, and Christmas came and went, and still no baby.

New Year's Eve was mild. Al and I stood on the porch for a few minutes after Mandy was in bed and wondered how long the warm spell would last.

We woke up to find snow to the top of the doorway. Snow covered every window in the cabin. Our car was buried. We couldn't see the top of it. Not even a hump. And me two weeks overdue!

Al spent the day trying to beat, shovel and flounder a path out. It was the only time I ever regretted living so far from the road.

I knew no one would try to come to tend Apples. The men often didn't bother on Sundays anyway. Undoubtedly, they felt we would feed him if they didn't.

I tried my best to reach the shed while Mandy was napping and Al was struggling to the road. In some places the snow was only knee deep, but in others I waded to my armpits. I got within 20 feet of the mill, when the snow defeated me. The drifts had blown in all around the little shed, and I just couldn't go any further. I was so tired and frustrated that I cried as I slowly and painfully groped back to the snug, warm cabin.

Toward evening, Al finished beating a path of sorts to Arthur's house. Soon after that, he got through the last deep drift to Apples. He came back in disgust. There wasn't a wafer of hay or a grain of feed up there; just a gaunt, shivering, hungry, thirsty horse.

Al waded out in the snow again. He borrowed Arthur's snowshoes and came back from the next farm with a bale of hay on his shoulders. I took the spare blanket from the bed and sent it up with a couple of diaper pins.

Three days later, the main roads were finally plowed. Just in time, too. Al had hitchhiked to work, leaving me with the snowshoes. I strapped them on, bundled Mandy onto her little toboggan and waded forth.

Arthur had his car dug out by the time I got there. We left Mandy with his wife, Ellie, and Arthur drove me to Bangor, stopping for Al on the way.

In the hospital, they took one look at me and said "Gee, lady, what's your hurry?" I kissed Al and whispered, "Please take good care of my horse." Two hours later, Jonathan was born.

Three days passed. We were home again. Still no sign of the pulp cutters. By this time, a bulldozer had cleared the lane to our cabin. From there, Al hauled water and feed to Apples on Mandy's toboggan. Soon I was helping him. We took turns the rest of the winter.

Often, when I entered the shed, Apples would whuff against my cheek, sigh, drop his huge head in my arms and go to sleep. I would brace against the shed wall to cradle his weight, breathe in the smell of horse and be at peace.

The snow got deeper, though never again did we get three feet in one night. We gave up being bulldozed out and left the car by the road. The weather was too rough for babies, so I didn't get much farther than Apples' shed all winter.

Spring came, despite my doubts. Mandy and Jonathan and I got out again. So did Apples. We turned him loose to go where he pleased. He was shedding. No matter how much I groomed him, he still itched. He found a couple of small alders that fit nicely under his belly, and he'd gyrate around on those like a fat lady doing the hula.

I hitched him up and put him to work now and then. Of course, I had never harnessed a horse before, and there was so much baling twine holding the harness together it didn't help me any to figure it out. I got the collar upside down the first time, but the hames wouldn't fit, so after a try or two I got straightened around.

First we hauled some old logs off from around our cabin, which gave us space for a larger yard. Then I tried twitching some new logs in from the woods.

I had a little back carrier for Jonathan. With the baby securely in that and Mandy by the hand, I led Apples into the woods, found a likely log (the pulp cutters had left plenty) and hooked him up.

Fearful that Mandy might be hurt when he lunged forward into the harness, I left the old horse there and led her down a bit, planted her firmly off the path with instructions to "wait," walked back for Apples and drove him up to where she was standing.

We did that twice. The third time, Apples started up as soon as Mandy and I stepped off the path, came to where we waited and stopped. I no longer bothered with reins.

He brought in new clothesline posts for Ellie and for me and enough logs for Al to build a small barn of our own.

In between times, we rode him. Mandy often sat in front of me, laughing and kicking and hanging on to his scraggly mane. Sometimes Al would hand me the baby and climb up behind. He could carry all four of us with ease and was content to walk up and down in front of the cabin all day, if that was what I wanted.

I am still not sure who really owned him. The pulp cutters owed the sales stable for him, and they had borrowed the down payment from Arthur, at that. No one wanted him but me, and I couldn't afford him. At length, an ad was placed in the paper to sell him.

You know, I swear the old horse had been sold so many times, he knew the routine. As kind and honest as he was, the minute someone came to look at him, he'd bare those old yellow teeth, pin his ears, lash out those bucket hooves and scare a buyer into the next county. He built a dandy reputation as an outlaw in two weeks. He was finally sold to the only place that would take him—the fox farm.

It was perhaps best. He was too old and too unsound to work in the woods anymore. At least he would never again be left to starve or be beaten with the blunt edge of an ax.

I cried when he left. I've had a lifetime of horses since, but none like him.

I didn't see him again, but I was told later the fox farm turned him out to pasture until fall. I hope so. He would have liked the summer.

Mary Harrison's 45-year tenure in the equine world has led her to fulfill a variety of roles including those of owner, active rider, 4-H leader, instructor and judge. She lives in Summer Shade, Kentucky.

"Apples stumbled into my life, and I into his, at a time when I badly

needed a sense of self and he needed a friend. If it were not for my experience with him, I might never have actually tried to own a horse.

"I regret that Apples was never mine, that I was helpless to give him the retirement he deserved. I had the old horse for a winter. He gave me a lifetime full of wonderful horses and horsepeople and serenity of soul. I owe him, and I love him still." —Mary Harrison

A Fan For Life

*Secretariat has been gone for
some time, but his many devoted admirers
continue to keep his memory alive.*

Cindy Tunstall

Secretariat has inspired many tributes over the years. Sportswriters, trainers, jockeys and many others have written eloquently about the great horse who captured the nation's imagination with his Triple Crown victory in 1973. This tribute comes from a fan who simply loved him and was lucky enough to see him in the flesh, just one time.

I purchased my first horse, a yearling colt, in 1973. He was an ordinary horse, full of himself and determined to get his way when he could. We called him Hot Shot, and in spite of his shortcomings, he was a dream come true for me—and the beginning of much more.

I had never paid much attention to the Kentucky Derby before, but as May approached, it was easy to get caught up in the excitement as my riding buddies started talking about the big race. Newly interested in everything related to horses, I eagerly sat before the television on race day and heard for the first time about a special colt named Secretariat. When the strapping chestnut, nicknamed "Big Red," came from behind to overpower his rivals and break the Derby record, something tugged inside me.

Though it was just two weeks later, the Preakness Stakes seemed too long in coming. I couldn't wait to see Secretariat run in the second leg of the Triple Crown. In that race, he had a sluggish start but then began passing horses as if they were moving in slow motion. I cheered the big red colt from my living-room couch until he swept under the finish wire. After that, I didn't doubt for a second that he would go on to win the Belmont Stakes and become the first horse in 25 years—since Citation in 1948—to win the Triple Crown.

Three weeks later, when the day of the Belmont Stakes arrived, I could hardly contain my excitement. I was at the barn with Hot Shot on that lovely June afternoon, and when it was time for the race, the stable owner called several of us into the main house so we could cheer on Secretariat together. Only four horses dared to compete against him for the final leg of the Triple Crown.

As post time approached, my heart was racing as I prayed for Secretariat. Prayed that he would win. Knew he would win. Knew he was that special horse destined for extraordinary feats. He didn't disappoint. He flew. He ran as if he knew that he was meant for greatness and this was his moment to show it. He finished the Belmont in a record time of 2:24 for the mile and a half, a track mark that still stands 22 years later, and he came under the wire 31 lengths in front of the second-place finisher, Twice A Prince. No horse in the history of the Belmont Stakes has ever won by such a huge margin or in a faster time.

I blinked back tears as Secretariat was led into the winner's circle. He looked so noble and beautiful. He was not my horse, yet that day he belonged to everyone. I didn't care if others were around to see me cry—I didn't see right away that they were crying, too. For those few precious moments, we all shared in Secretariat's greatness.

Secretariat competed in several more races during 1973, and after his final victory in Canada that October, he was retired to stud at Claiborne Farm in Paris, Kentucky.

In the years after Secretariat's departure from the racetrack, I never missed a Triple Crown race. I hoped every year to see a film clip of him, another chance to savor his standard-setting victories. But, understandably, the broadcasts usually focused on the current contenders rather than revisiting the past, however glorious it was. Then one Christmas, wrapped up and under the tree, was a special present from my husband. Unknown to me, he had contacted all of the tracks—Churchill Downs, Pimlico Racecourse and Belmont Park—and bought videotapes of each of Secretariat's Triple Crown races.

But the best present came a few years later.

In 1985, my husband came home from work one day and told me he had to go to Kentucky to do a newspaper story about the Thoroughbred industry. He had an interview set up at Claiborne Farm. My heart pounded. Did he think, did I dare hope that I could see Secretariat? Was it possible? It was.

Sitting in the office of Claiborne's farm manager, John Sosby, I tried to be quiet while my husband asked questions. Finally, the interview drew to a close, and I was able to ask Sosby about Secretariat. He was happy to oblige, speaking with pride and fondness about the stallion. We talked about "Red," about how John had reacted the same way I did when he won. How it still gives me gooseflesh thinking about the moment. And writing about it now.

He gave me one of Secretariat's horseshoes and, to this day, I don't know of anything that has moved me more. Then he took me to see Red. The stallion had been grazing at the back of his paddock but galloped up to the fence where we were standing. He was many years older and more than a few pounds heavier than in his days of glory, but Secretariat still looked like the magnificent champion he was. I will never forget the thrill of running my hands along his strong neck, across his broad shoulders and over his still muscular chest. Thinking back, I can still feel his strength, the silky smoothness of his shining coat and the beating of his heart. Since that day, I have met many great men and women in my travels as a writer and photographer, but none has impressed me more than that big chestnut stallion.

Four years later, on October 4, 1989, Secretariat was humanely destroyed to spare him the ravages of laminitis. That night, television newscasts showed him running about in his paddock. As I watched, I remembered the day he ran to me. My heart broke—for John Sosby, for Secretariat's fans, for myself and, most of all, for Big Red.

Today, I still watch the Triple Crown races, but now it's to make sure no horse beats his record—and to see whether one of his grandchildren is blessed with his gift. Secretariat's horseshoe hangs in a place of honor in my home, affixed to a plaque designed to hold it. Next to it are photographs of the stallion alone and one with me in the picture. The biggest is a print that is titled "The Last Portrait." It was taken October 3, 1989, the day before he died.

He lives on on that wall. And in my heart. And in many others.

At one time a devoted English pleasure and hunt-seat rider, Cindy Tunstall says her favorite equestrian endeavor in recent year has been trail riding near her Lecanto, Florida, home.

"In 1997, I traveled back to Claiborne Farm to visit Secretariat's grave. Bouquets of yellow mums and red roses left by someone before me lay around his granite marker. I left my tears and a small gold pin of a colt, along with a wish that one day his gift would be passed onto a worthy foal so that we would see greatness again."—Cindy Tunstall

Home For Christmas

*Against the odds and the
elements, a jockey helps make the holidays happy
for a struggling racetrack family.*

JAN JASION CROSS

It was some kind of cosmic thing that took me there. I certainly did not go for the money or the atmosphere. Pocono Downs in late November was, in fact, quite depressing—the temperatures averaged about 25 degrees by post time for the first race each evening. Plus there was a nice, comfortable job waiting for me in Florida for the winter months. A leading New York trainer had offered me a position as an assistant trainer and exercise girl. It was a job I had prayed for. I finally had fallen on my head enough times to realize that my waning career as a jockey was becoming more dangerous than lucrative.

I would have gone straight to Florida and strolled the sunny, blessed beaches for a few weeks while I waited for the New York outfit if I hadn't gotten sidetracked by two of my best friends. Russ and Jackie were a hardworking young couple, and I had won a few races on their cheaper horses at a Philadelphia track. They were heading to Florida too. But first they were going to ship part of their stable to Pocono Downs, in Wilkes-Barre, Pennsylvania, to win some races and lose some of their cheap claimers, horses who compete in races in which all entries are for sale at a specified price. Somehow, they convinced me that I should accompany them. We were staying only for a few weeks, they told me, and we would win lots of races. I packed halfheartedly.

We shipped in one afternoon the week before Thanksgiving. The roads were becoming slick from the falling sleet. Our little caravan slid through the stable gate and down a hill that bottomed out at our assigned barn. My little car had no snow tires. If it had, I probably would have made a quick U-turn and headed south, but there was no way my car was going to make it back up that hill. We unloaded the horses from the van and headed for the little apartment that we would share for three weeks, sipping hot chocolate laced with whiskey and dreaming of the big bets we would cash.

I had made a pact with myself not to ride for any trainer at Pocono Downs but Russ. There was that job waiting for me in Florida, and I did not want to risk getting on horses I did not know for trainers I did not know. But pacts were made to be broken.

Stabled next to Russ and Jackie's string at barn "T" was an odd sort of outfit. The Boyd racing stable had traveled to Pocono Downs from a little track out West. A few days after our own arrival, their battered old Ford pickup had chugged in, toting a rusty two-horse trailer. The entire stable consisted of two aged geldings. The two old warhorses received plenty of attention, for the trainer, Sally, was accompanied by her husband, elderly father and young son. The little boy, Scott, was a towheaded, courteous and attentive 11-year-old. I asked how it was that he got to skip school and live at the racetrack with his folks. Scott told me that just as soon as the family could get some money together, they would be going home for Christmas. Then he would return to school. Home, Scott told me, was in Arkansas.

Sensing that the Boyd stable could not afford an exercise rider, I volunteered to gallop their two-horse stable for them. Sally readily accepted my offer. One horse, Bart, galloped an easy mile every morning, but the other horse, a black gelding named Coaly, was a wee bit off in the left ankle and usually was ponied alongside Russ' stable pony for his daily exercise.

Within hours of arriving at the track, little Scott asked Russ and Jackie if he could work for them for wages. I am sure that Russ had no clue as to what duties Scott would perform, but he did not hesitate in putting the little boy on his payroll. From then on, Scott hustled about the barn all morning, cheerfully holding horses for baths, bedding stalls, raking the shed row and helping me clean tack. Russ paid his little right-hand man his wages daily. Scott would thank him politely and hurry off to join his folks down the shed row. The entire clan would then stroll over to the track kitchen for breakfast. I don't think they ever left the racetrack grounds.

Three weeks went by, and my calendar was lined with X's that ended with the date of my departure for Florida. By December 15, Russ had run and lost the last horse he wanted to part with. He was making shipping arrangements, and I was planning to get my gear out of the jocks' room and settle up with my valet, Paul. Our neighbors down the shed row had not yet raced Coaly or Bart.

On the 16th, I went to the jocks' room after morning workouts to retrieve my belongings. But when I requested my tack, Paul gave me a look of consternation. "You can't leave," he said. "You have a mount tonight in the ninth race." He pulled a folded list of the day's entries from his back pocket and passed it to me. He was right. I was named on "Coal Bay" in the ninth. I asked Paul if he had seen the form on Coaly. "Uh-huh. If this horse wins tonight, there are snowmen in Hell," he replied. "Gonna take off?"

I nearly let the word "yes" slip through my badly chapped lips when I caught sight of something out of the corner of my eye. It was little Scott. The racetrack cherub had come dashing out of the racing secretary's office with the entries list in his hand. He was jumping up and down like a young antelope as he raced back to the barn area. "No," I said. "I guess I'm riding tonight."

That evening, before dinner, I borrowed Russ' *Daily Racing Form* to study Coal Bay's past performances. He had not seen a winner's circle since he was seven, and he would be nine years old in a few weeks. The chart writer had summed up Coaly's last three efforts as "dull," "outdistanced" and "tired early." These performances had been in cheap claiming races. Tonight Coaly was entered in an allowance race, a higher level of competition.

At 6:30 I went to the jocks' room to await my last ride at Pocono Downs. God, was it cold out! As I donned my riding garb, I thought to myself that riding a 60-to-1 shot on a night of freezing temperatures was not a terrific way to end one's race-riding career. Such was fate. When the call went round the jocks' room for the ninth race weigh-in, my valet informed me that it was 10 degrees outside. I put on an extra-heavy turtleneck shirt after weigh-in and stuck my gloves and boots into the sauna for a last-minute toasting before venturing out.

In the paddock, my teeth chattered as Sally told me that Coaly was a cold-weather horse. The old gelding did look good. His coat was thick and shiny. His large hazel eyes were bright with anticipation. I glanced over at our competition. One horse stood out: The betting favorite, Fast Exit, had just shipped in from New Jersey, but I knew him well. I had ridden Fast Exit when he won his first race a couple years before at a Jersey Shore track. With that race, I lost my "bug," the weight allowance given to apprentice riders until they chalk up a certain number of victories, and the trainer I was riding for promptly fired me. Another memorable day in my career. The same trainer still saddled Fast Exit, and I waved stiffly at him as he met my stare. Suddenly, Coaly and I had a mission. We had to beat Fast Exit, for old times' sake.

When the gates opened, Coaly shot out like a bolt of black lightning. We easily took the lead, with Fast Exit alongside. My old Coaly was running like a fine-tuned sports car. In fact, Fast Exit seemed to be having trouble keeping up. I signaled to Coaly, and we easily left the favorite in the dust. From the quarter pole to the wire we raced along, just me and Coal Bay. At the eighth pole, I started grinning and posing. To the wire we coasted, four lengths ahead of the favorite.

Coaly pulled up kindly and galloped back to the winner's circle like a gentleman. He was my hero, and I patted his glistening neck tenderly as we posed for the picture. Sally, her husband, father and little Scott were surprisingly calm during the brief victory ceremony. "We knew he could do it!" Scott declared. I thanked them all for a most memorable ride.

The next morning, I went to the stables at 8. I was packed and ready to head to Florida. But before I hit the highway, I needed to see my new friends one last time. I headed over to the two stalls where Coal Bay and his stablemate had been bedded. The stalls were empty. I was quite upset to find the Boyd stable gone without notice. Russ walked down the shed row and stood by my side as I stared misty-eyed at Coal Bay's empty stall. "They were already gone when I got here this morning. They must have loaded up in the middle of the night," he said. "I think something was left for you on their tack-room door."

I walked slowly to the end of the shed and pulled the piece of white construction paper from the door. It was a crayon drawing depicting a huge black horse in a winner's circle; his jockey had been given a large red nose like that of Rudolph the Red-Nosed Reindeer. A family of four was grouped at the horse's head.

I smiled as I read the neatly hand-printed caption at the bottom of the picture: "COAL BAY—WINNER—WE ARE GOING HOME FOR CHRISTMAS," and, in smaller letters, "Thanks Jan. We love you, [signed] Scott." Only then did I realize why I had come to Pocono Downs.

Jan Jasion Cross has spent a large portion of the last 40 years working with Thoroughbred racehorses. Among other positions, she has worked as an exercise rider, jockey, trainer, owner and breeding-farm manager. The summer of 1997 found her training and riding at Thistledown Racetrack in Cleveland.

Illustrations by Pamela Wildermuth